GOOD★SPORTS

BY GLENN STOUT

YES,
SHE
CAN!

GOOD SPORTS

BY GLENN STOUT

YES,
SHE
CAN!

WOMEN'S SPORTS PIONEERS

sandpiper

HOUGHTON MIFFLIN HARCOURT
BOSTON NEW YORK 2011

www.hmhbooks.com

The text of this book is set in ITC Slimbach.

Jacket art © 2011 Cover photographs: Danica Patrick photo © 2010 Associated
Press/Shuji Kajiyama; Tidye Pickett and Louise Stokes photo © Associated
Press; Julie Krone photo © Associated Press/Mark Lennihan; Trudy Ederle
photo © Keystone View Co.

Library of Congress Cataloging-in-Publication Data

Stout, Glenn, 1958–

Yes she can!: women's sports pioneers/by Glenn Stout.

p. cm.—(Good sports ; 2)

ISBN 978-0-547-41725-7

1. Women athletes—Biography. 2. Sports for women—History. I. Title.

GV697.A1S74 2011

796.0922 dc22

2010022984

Manufactured the United States of America
DOC 10 9 8 7 6 5 4 3 2 1

4500285029

This book is dedicated to

Saorla Stout,

Piper Dean,

Ainsley Dean,

and all my other young friends
and readers who are "Good Sports"

CONTENTS

INTRODUCTION...

TRUDY'S BIG SPLASH.......................

THE REAL WINNERS.......................

RACING AHEAD............................

YOUNG WOMAN IN A HURRY...............

SOURCES AND FURTHER READING.........

APPENDIX.................................

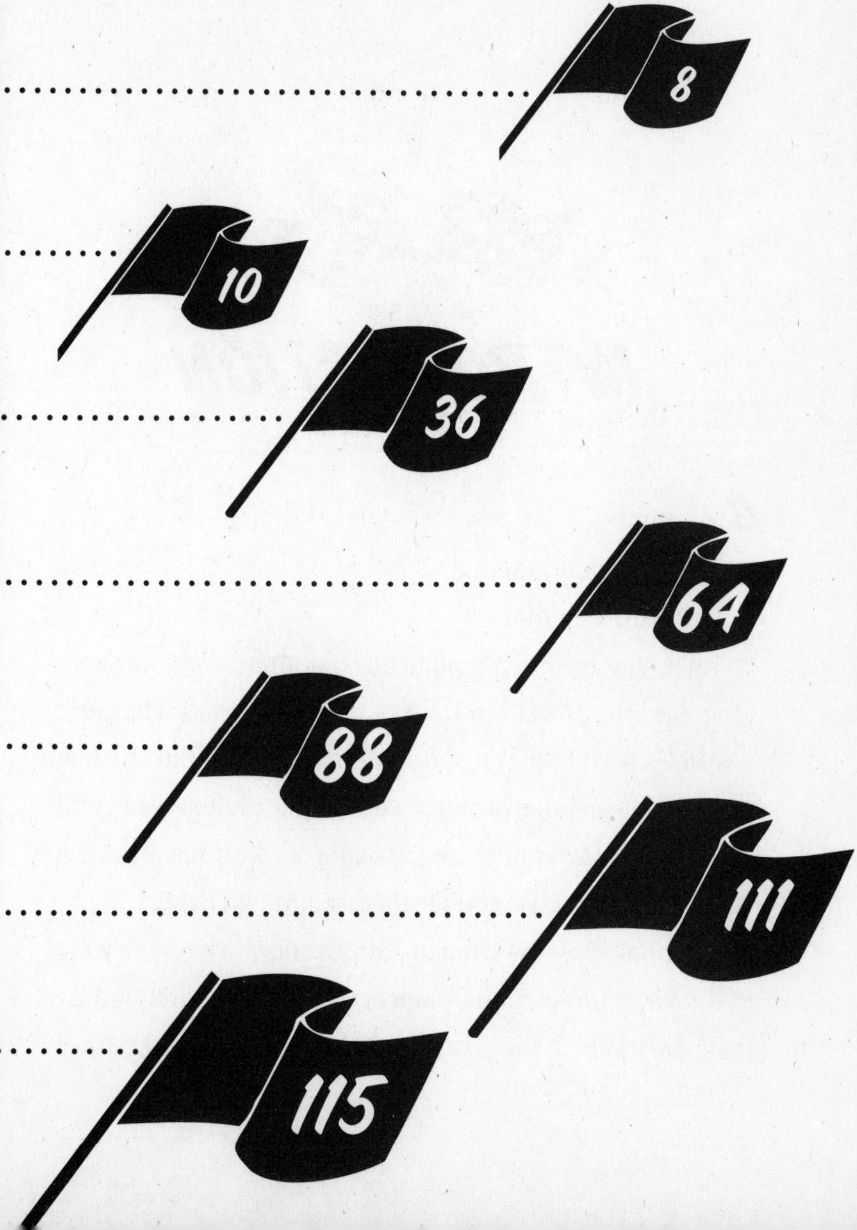
8
10
36
64
88
111
115

INTRODUCTION

*G*irls don't do that.

Girls shouldn't do that.

Girls *can't* do that.

Have you ever heard someone say that? Well, not very long ago, that's exactly what many people said whenever a woman tried to play a sport or do anything athletic. Most people believed that women were physically too weak and delicate to play sports. There might as well have been a sign at the gymnasium door that said MEN ONLY.

Fortunately, some women didn't believe what they were told. When these sports pioneers were told "Girls don't," they did. When they were told "Girls shouldn't," they asked "Why not?" And when they were told "Girls can't," they became more determined than ever. This book tells the stories of several pioneers in women's sports, all of whom refused to be told what they could and could not do. And because they proved that girls can do *anything,* women today compete in sports of all kinds, from track and field, figure skating, and swimming to tackle football and racecar driving. Sports not only provide good exercise, they also help participants gain self-confidence and learn to work together and set goals.

It took some remarkable women to show everyone else the way. That's what Gertrude "Trudy" Ederle, Louise Stokes, Tidye Pickett, Julie Krone, and Danica Patrick all have in common. When these girls were told they could not do something, they made even those who had doubted them say, "Yes, she can!"

A smiling Trudy Ederle practices swimming in the English Channel.

TRUDY'S BIG SPLASH

ON THE MORNING OF AUGUST 6, 1926, an editorial appeared in the *London Daily News* about the rights of women to compete in and play sports. The editorial ended, "Even the most uncompromising champion of the rights of women must admit that in contests of physical skill, speed, and endurance, they must forever remain the weaker sex." As residents of London read the paper over their morning tea, a young American woman named Trudy Ederle stood on the shore in France and looked out across the English Channel toward England, twenty-one miles away.

Although dozens and dozens of people had tried to swim the English Channel before, only five — all men — had made it across. Swimming the Channel is one of the most difficult and dangerous athletic feats in the world. Even today, more people have climbed Mount Everest than have swum the English Channel. In 1875, Matthew Webb became the first person to swim the Channel, a feat that took him nearly twenty-two hours to accomplish. The speed record was held by the third person to swim the Channel, Enrique Tirabocci, who in 1923 made the crossing in sixteen hours and thirty-three minutes.

Although many had tried, no woman had ever swum the English Channel. A few had made it within a few miles of the opposite shore before bad weather, fatigue, and tides forced them out of the water, and many more quit after only a few hours in the water. In 1925, in fact, Trudy Ederle had tried to swim the Channel only to fail. Although she had been considered the greatest female swimmer in the world at the time, many observers thought that if Trudy could not swim the Channel, then no woman could.

Trudy disagreed and decided to try again. Now, just a few minutes after seven a.m., she adjusted her swimming goggles and stepped into the water. When the waves reached her chest, she took a deep breath, looked up at the sun peeking through the hazy summer sky, and whispered, "God, help me." Then, with a big splash, she dove beneath the waves and started swimming.

Trudy was determined to succeed this time. She knew that a woman could swim the English Channel.

All she had to do was prove it.

In the summer of 1915, Trudy's father, Henry, purchased a small cottage near the beach in Highlands, New Jersey. The Ederle family lived in New York City, where Henry owned and operated a successful butcher shop. Henry and his wife, Gertrud, thought their children—Helen, age twelve; Meg, age ten; Trudy, age nine; and Emma and George, both toddlers—would enjoy spending the summers out of the city.

Highlands was beautiful. Trudy loved gazing out over the water, the sea breeze blowing through her light brown hair and the sun bringing out the freckles on her face. There were plenty of children her age to play with, but Trudy, who was partially deaf due to a bout with the measles a few years before, was a little shy. She sometimes couldn't understand what strangers were saying and occasionally felt embarrassed when meeting new people, so she followed her older sisters Helen and Meg around like a puppy. Nearly every day they all went to the beach together.

That was the problem. Helen and Meg knew how to swim. Trudy did not. When Helen and Meg went in the water, Trudy had to stay behind, playing alone in the sand and wading in the shallows.

It seems hard to believe today, but a hundred years ago, very few women knew how to swim, and few were allowed to compete in sports of any kind. When women went to the beach, they were expected to wear long-sleeved blouses and stockings that made swimming next to impossible. There were virtually no swimming pools with lifeguards, no groups like the YWCA that gave swimming lessons, and no girls' swim teams or swim meets for young girls to compete in. Trudy's sisters only knew how to swim because they had been taught the dog paddle and the breaststroke by their cousins when the family had visited relatives in Germany. Trudy had been too young to learn, and now she felt left out.

Henry Ederle, however, had a solution. One day he went to the beach with the girls and told Helen and Meg to get in the water. As Trudy stood on the beach, Henry took a strong piece of clothesline and tied it around her chest. He walked out onto a nearby pier and told Trudy to wade toward her sisters.

Trudy took a few cautious steps and suddenly her feet no longer touched bottom. As a panicked look came over her face and she began to sink, her father pulled on the rope, keeping Trudy on the surface. Then Meg and Helen urged her to paddle toward them.

At first Trudy did little more than thrash about while taking in great gulps of air before grabbing one of her sisters for support. But each time she let go and tried to swim from one sister to the other, she became a bit more confident and relaxed. Soon she could feel her body floating in the water. She forgot all about the rope and didn't even notice that her father had let it go slack.

Trudy was swimming. And she loved it. For some reason, as she floated in the water alone with her thoughts, Trudy felt more at home than anywhere else in the world. As she later explained, "To me, the sea is like a person—like a child that I've known a long time. It sounds crazy, I know, but when I swim in the sea I talk to it. I never feel alone when I'm out there." For the rest of her life, the sea would be her best friend. Trudy spent most of every day the family stayed in Highlands swimming in the sea.

One summer day a few years later, Trudy's mother took her daughters to one of the piers along the water. She had seen a notice for a demonstration held by a group called the Women's Swimming Association (WSA). She thought her daughters, who all loved to swim, might want to watch.

The Ederle girls were amazed by what they saw. At the

start of the show, a half dozen or so young women stood on the pier and started diving into the water. They didn't do cannonballs, as did many young men who sometimes liked to show off. One after another they jumped into the air, arched their bodies in flight, and entered the water straight as an arrow, hardly making a splash. It was like watching ballet.

After the diving demonstration, a young girl only five or six years old jumped into the water and started to swim to a nearby pier. She didn't use the dog paddle or the breaststroke like Trudy and her sisters. Instead, she reached out with first one arm and then the other while her feet kicked like mad. She moved across the water so fast that it almost looked as if she were crawling on the surface.

The stroke she used was called the American crawl, now a common stroke more often referred to as freestyle. But when Trudy was a little girl, the crawl, which had only been invented a few years before, was rarely seen outside of men's athletic clubs. Trudy and her sisters had occasionally seen young men use the stroke in Highlands, but they had never dreamed that a girl could learn to swim that way.

When the demonstration was over, one of the founders

of the WSA, Charlotte Epstein, spoke to the small crowd. She explained that she had created the organization for the health and safety of women. Swimming was not only fun and good exercise, but it was also a skill that could save lives. Each year, she explained, women all over the world drowned because they did not know how to swim.

In the crowd, heads bobbed up and down in agreement. Many of the adults remembered a boating accident in New York years earlier when a big steamship, the *General Slocum*, caught fire and ran aground. The boat had been only a few yards from shore, but nearly a thousand women and children had drowned.

Epstein went on to explain that for only a few dollars a year, members of the WSA could take weekly swimming lessons and learn the crawl. As swimmers improved, they could compete in races and demonstrations sponsored by the WSA. The best swimmers might even become instructors and teach other girls and women to swim.

Trudy's mother looked at her daughters. The girls were mesmerized. She could tell what they were thinking.

When Charlotte Epstein invited members of the crowd to join the group, Gertrud ushered her daughters to the front. "I'll give you a thousand dollars," she blurted out, "if you can teach my girls to swim like that."

Charlotte Epstein just laughed and signed the girls up. The WSA had three new recruits.

For the next few years, Helen, Meg, and Trudy traveled once each week to the WSA pool for their lessons. During the summer the WSA used an outdoor pool near the seashore filled with seawater; during the winter they met at an indoor pool in the basement of an apartment building. The lessons were run by the only man in the group, WSA swim coach Louis de Breda Handley. Handley had invented the American crawl and was one of the best swimming teachers in the world.

Of the three sisters, Meg was the most dedicated and, at first, the most athletic and talented. She learned quickly and was soon competing in races.

Trudy, on the other hand, didn't seem too promising. In fact, the first time Trudy swam in the pool, one of the other instructors told Coach Handley that she was "too wild" in the water and suggested that they steer her toward the diving team. But Handley was patient with his students, and ever so slowly, Trudy began to improve. She just liked to swim and didn't care much about competing. Unless Meg signed her up for a race, she didn't even bother with it. During summers in Highlands, she hardly went to the WSA pool at all. Instead, she spent hours each day at the beach, swimming for her own pleasure.

Late in the summer of 1922, when Trudy was fifteen, Meg entered a three-mile race in the open ocean off Long Island. A famous swimmer from England, Hilda James, was scheduled to compete, as were the best swimmers in the WSA. At the last minute, Meg talked Trudy into entering the race as well.

The girls were ferried out to the starting point, and as they spread out, all eyes were on Hilda James and the WSA's best swimmers, Helen Wainwright, Ethel McGary, and Aileen Riggin. James, Wainwright, and Riggin had all swum in the 1920 Olympic Games. Everyone watching from boats offshore expected either James or one of the veteran WSA swimmers to win.

At the start, James and the three WSA swimmers slowly pulled away from the pack on one side of the course. After a few minutes, an official noticed that another swimmer way over on the other side of the course, all by herself, was already several yards ahead of everyone, including James.

Observers pulled out binoculars and squinted at the splashing figure. "It's that Ederle girl," someone called.

Officials from the WSA looked at one another in surprise. Meg Ederle was a very good swimmer, but no one had expected her to challenge for the lead. Then another voice rang out. "It's not Meg...it's Trudy!"

No one could believe it. Trudy hardly ever competed, but all that time she spent swimming in Highlands had made her strong. With each stroke, Trudy Ederle was pulling farther ahead. She was thrashing some of the best swimmers in the world! While they struggled, she just kept plowing through the water as if she didn't have a care in the world.

For the next hour, Trudy kept pulling ahead, and she finished the race an incredible forty-five seconds ahead of Helen Wainwright. When Trudy stepped out of the water, she was suddenly one of the best swimmers in the world, and one of the best known. Even James admitted to a reporter that "The best girl won. Of that I have no doubt."

In the wake of her win, Coach Handley began paying a little more attention to Trudy. Urged on by Meg, Trudy began entering swim meets.

Her performances were stunning. For the next two years, it seemed she set another world record nearly every time she went into the water. And she was just as good at short distances as she was at long races. By the time the

1924 Summer Olympics approached, Trudy was expected to be a big winner.

Trudy wanted to win, too. Swimming and diving were two of only a handful of Olympic sports open to women. At the 1924 Games in Paris, Trudy planned to compete in the 100-meter freestyle, the 400-meter freestyle, and the 4x100-meter relay. Louis Handley was the swim coach for the American women, and when Trudy and the rest of the team left by boat for Europe on July 16, 1924, Trudy was confident that she would do well.

But nothing went right for her. During the ten-day ocean journey, it was almost impossible for Trudy to train. On the ship, the team had to take turns swimming in place in a tiny pool only ten feet square. After they arrived in Paris, Trudy discovered that the entire team, men and women, had only one half hour per day for practice. Even worse, it took hours of travel in cramped cars and buses to reach the pool. By the time the competition began, Trudy was out of shape.

Instead of returning to the United States with three gold medals, she returned with only one, in the relay race. She had won bronze medals in the 100-meter and 400-meter individual freestyle races. She was proud of her accomplishments, but she still felt as if she had let everyone down. She later called the experience "the greatest disappointment of my life." At age seventeen, with another Olympics four long years away, Trudy wasn't sure what she would do next.

Her WSA and Olympic teammate Helen Wainwright was also wondering what to do after the Olympics. In recent years several men had swum the English Channel. Each successful swim attracted a great deal of attention, and soon afterward, a number of women had announced that they intended to become the first woman to swim the Channel. But none of these other swimmers, male or female, had tried to cross the Channel using the American crawl. Coach Handley had long thought that a woman swimming the crawl just might be able to set a new record. When Helen Wainwright indicated that she wanted to try, the WSA decided to sponsor her. They would pay for her travel to the Channel and for the several months of training a serious attempt would require.

Unfortunately for Helen, she pulled a muscle in her leg. When Trudy's sister Meg heard about that, she raced to the pool where Trudy was working out and, still dressed in her street clothes, called her younger sister over to the side.

In a rush she explained that Helen was hurt and told Trudy that now she absolutely, positively, no doubt about it, had to swim the Channel instead. After all, Meg said to Trudy, "If Helen Wainwright can swim five miles, you can swim six. Why don't you go?"

Trudy looked at her older sister. "Margaret," she said, calling her sister by her full name. "Are you crazy?"

Then Meg got to work. For the next few minutes she pushed and prodded and argued until she was almost out of breath. And the more she talked, the more Trudy came to realize that it would be impossible for her to say no. When Meg wanted her to do something, well, that was that.

"Okay," Trudy said, finally giving in. "Okay. Whatever you think." Then she turned around and started swimming. If she was going to swim the English Channel, she had a lot of work to do.

Helen Wainwright soon withdrew from the trip, and the WSA agreed to send Trudy instead. All winter long Trudy swam lap after lap after lap, building her strength and endurance. In June of 1925, Trudy and a chaperone sailed for England. The WSA hired a trainer, Jabez Wolffe, to supervise her effort. Although Wolffe had never swum the Channel himself, he had tried more than twenty times and knew all about the cold, treacherous Channel waters.

Wolffe's firsthand knowledge was important, because it takes more to swim the Channel than just the ability to swim twenty-one miles. It also takes planning. Strong tides and currents make it impossible to swim straight across. Instead, swimmers must zigzag across, riding the tides, sometimes swimming thirty or forty miles in the process. The water is bone-chillingly cold, rarely rising above sixty degrees, and the weather over the Channel can change unexpectedly. A day that begins with blue skies and calm waters can end in a full-blown gale powerful enough to sink ships, and the sun is often blocked out by dense fog. Many Channel swimmers have come within a mile or two of success only to be defeated by a combination of weather conditions, water temperature, strong tides, and fatigue. Swimming across the English Channel is one of the most difficult feats of endurance in the world.

Wolffe knew all about that—the Channel had defeated him more often than any other swimmer in history. Although he agreed to train Trudy, he didn't really believe she could succeed, at least not using the crawl. He tried to convince her to abandon the crawl in favor of the breaststroke, but Trudy refused. She and Wolffe simply did not get along.

By the time Trudy entered the water at Cape Gris-Nez in France on August 17, 1925, she and Wolffe were hardly speaking. Although the weather was fine at first, almost from the very start of her swim, Trudy didn't feel right. She felt sick to her stomach and was tired, as if she had already spent the day swimming.

Nevertheless, for the first six hours she swam strongly. Wolffe followed her in a rowboat, and a tugboat stayed nearby in case it was needed. Then the weather changed and the sea became rough. Midafternoon, as another swimmer swam next to Trudy to keep her company, Trudy swallowed some water. She stopped swimming for a moment and rolled over on her back. "Take her out," snapped Wolffe. "That's enough." The other swimmer touched Trudy and helped her back into the boat. According to the rules that govern Channel swimming, a swimmer cannot be touched in the water. Trudy's swim was over.

Trudy was bitterly disappointed. She blamed Wolffe for making her stop and eventually came to believe that he — or someone else — had put something in her drinks that made her sleepy. The WSA fired Wolffe and hired another trainer, Bill Burgess, the second man ever to swim the

Channel. Trudy liked him much better, but the weather turned bad, and after a few weeks she had to return to the United States.

Still, Trudy did not give up on her dream of swimming the Channel. Over the next few months, she talked with her family about trying again. When the WSA balked at the cost of sponsoring a second attempt, Trudy began teaching swimming. Then a newspaper made the decision to sponsor Trudy in exchange for the rights to her story. She began to plan another attempt at the Channel for the summer of 1926.

This time she would be in control. Both her father and Meg accompanied her to Europe, and they all stayed in the same hotel in Cape Gris-Nez, France, where Trudy decided to start her swim again. She got along much better with Bill Burgess than she ever had with Wolffe. He didn't try to change the way she swam and was usually very supportive. He had spent years studying the tides and currents in the Channel and thought he had figured out the best route across.

In the weeks before Trudy was scheduled to make her attempt, she and Meg had some work to do. During her first attempt, Trudy had been bothered by both her swimsuit and her goggles. Her one-piece swimsuit had irritated her skin and slowed her down, and her goggles had leaked badly. Now, she and Meg started experimenting.

To keep the suit from irritating her skin, they cut a silk one-piece suit into two pieces, a top and a bottom. Trudy found the new suit far more comfortable. She and her sister did not realize it, but they had just invented the first bikini.

Her goggles, however, were still a problem. No matter what they tried, salt water still leaked in around the lens and irritated her eyes. But one evening a few days before she was supposed to swim the Channel, Trudy stared at the wax dripping down a candle. "Gee, Meg," she wondered aloud, "maybe we should melt a candle on the inside of the goggles!" The girls gathered some candles and carefully dripped wax around the edge of the glass on the goggles. The next day, Trudy went for a swim. When she got out of the water, she walked toward her sister with a huge grin on her face. "Meg, I think we have them waterproof!"

Later, she went for a long walk down the beach with Meg and their father. Trudy was still upset at having been taken out of the water the previous summer and told her father, "Remember, don't let anyone take me out of the water." Her father promised.

Later that day, Bill Burgess told Trudy that if the weather stayed calm, she would start the swim at seven o'clock the following morning. The problems with her suit and her goggles had been solved, she had her family with her for support, and she had a trainer she trusted. Trudy was ready. Before she went to bed, she told the crowd in the hotel dining room, "England or die. That's my motto!" Then she went to sleep.

Meg woke Trudy at dawn. "Do we go?" she asked her sister. Meg nodded and Trudy got ready for her swim, donning her suit and eating a light breakfast. She then went by car to the beach, where Bill Burgess coated her body with several coats of thick, sticky grease. The covering would help keep her warm and prevent the salt water from chafing her skin.

It looked to be a fine day. The water was calm and the skies were clear, although the sun had to fight to burn through the morning haze. As several dozen newspapermen and onlookers stood on the beach, Burgess and Meg climbed into a rowboat and began rowing out to sea, where a larger tug that would escort Trudy across the Channel waited a few hundred yards offshore. Her father was already onboard, as were several other swimmers who hoped to swim the Channel one day and had volunteered to keep her company.

"I'll make it this time," Trudy said to the crowd. Then, holding her sticky arms away from her body, she laughed and said, "I feel just like a greaseball."

Then she took a few deep breaths and walked into the water. She thought for a moment about the red roadster automobile her father had promised to buy for her if she made it across, then looked up and whispered a quiet prayer. Then she dove beneath a wave and started to swim. If everything worked out, her next step would be on the English shore, twenty-one miles in the distance.

The water was cold, but by now Trudy was accustomed to it. For a few minutes she struggled to find a comfortable pace, but then she settled in to her preferred speed of twenty-eight strokes per minute. Before she had left, Coach Handley had made her promise to use the crawl stroke the entire way. He told her that if she did, he thought she could make it across in about fourteen hours — if the weather held.

Trudy drew alongside the tug, and it rumbled to life. Making sure not to get in Trudy's way, the captain piloted the ship beside her. When Trudy turned her head, she could see her father, Meg, and Bill Burgess on the rail, watching over her. On the side of the ship, Meg had written in chalk "This way Ole Girl," with a big arrow pointing forward. Trudy laughed and kept swimming.

After a short time she heard singing: "Yes, we have no bananas, we have no bananas today." To help Trudy stay on pace and not get bored, Meg was playing records on the gramophone aboard the tug. On her previous attempt, Trudy had hired musicians to play, but they had all gotten seasick. This time, she wasn't taking any chances.

For the first three or four hours the swim was uneventful. Then Bill Burgess noticed that the weather was beginning to change. A southwest wind started to blow and the skies turned gray. The tug—and Trudy—rose up and down as large waves began to form.

Nevertheless, Trudy kept swimming. For a time, Meg joined her in the water, and the two sisters kept up a steady chatter as they swam. A short time after Meg left the water, another swimmer joined Trudy.

Just after noon, she paused for lunch. As she floated on her back, Bill Burgess first lowered a bottle of warm chicken broth attached to a line, then a chicken leg. As soon as she finished eating, Trudy started swimming again.

Bill Burgess was worried. It started to rain, and the captain began receiving reports from other ships that were running into poor weather. Some of the passengers aboard the boat were getting seasick. Burgess began to think that if the weather was going to continue to deteriorate, it might be better for Trudy to stop now, before she got too exhausted, and try the swim again in a few days.

Even as the wind-driven waves grew and the rain began pounding down, Trudy was unconcerned. She had always enjoyed swimming in poor weather — she actually considered it good luck. She felt strong and despite the weather hadn't slowed her pace at all. She was more than half-way across the Channel, and although she knew she would have a hard time fighting the tides the rest of the way, she still felt confident.

But with every passing minute, Bill Burgess grew more worried. He was afraid that Trudy might get swept under by a wave, swallow water, and drown, or that the tug would lose track of her as it began to grow dark. The tide was starting to change, and he no longer believed it was possible for any swimmer — even Trudy — to make it to the Dover shore.

Burgess approached Henry Ederle and told him of his concerns, but Trudy's father remembered his promise and refused to let his daughter be taken from the water. The two men began arguing on deck and were soon joined by the boat's captain. The captain agreed with Burgess. The other passengers began to choose sides, and soon everyone was arguing.

Trudy had no idea any of this was happening. Although she knew her progress against the tide had slowed, she felt fresh. Besides, she knew that the tide would soon shift again. There was no doubt in her mind that she would make it to England. At times, even as it was beginning to get dark, she could see the famous White Cliffs of Dover on the horizon.

All of a sudden someone on the boat — no one was ever quite sure who — cupped their hands around their mouth and yelled to Trudy.

"Come on out, girl, come out! Come out of the water!"

Although Trudy was hard of hearing, she still made out the voice booming over the water, calling for her to quit. She could hardly believe it. She felt fine. Besides, she wanted that red roadster, and she had told everyone she would rather drown than quit.

She stopped swimming for a moment, rolled onto her back, and looked at the tug. Everyone was crowded over the rail, looking at her, gesturing and arguing.

Trudy thought the whole thing was just plain silly. She turned her head and called out, "What for?"

Instantly, everyone stopped talking. Even though the waves were approaching six feet, rain was pouring down, and the wind was blowing nearly thirty miles an hour, the only person not bothered by the bad weather was Trudy. Why should she stop? "What for?" indeed.

No one had an answer to her question, and Trudy soon rolled back onto her belly and started swimming again. The captain went back to the pilothouse, Bill Burgess stayed quiet, and Trudy's father and sister shared a knowing look.

Ever so slowly, stroke by stroke, over the next few hours, Trudy swam the crawl toward England. As the sky turned dark and the boat shined a spotlight on her in the water, she began to sense the excitement on shore. Residents of the coast had learned of her attempt, and now the beaches were crowded with people. Some lit bonfires as searchlights crisscrossed the water trying to find her, and others fired red and blue flares that illuminated the night sky.

Just after nine o'clock p.m. it became clear that, barring catastrophe, Trudy would make it. Everyone forgot the arguments of earlier in the day. Even the sea calmed down.

Bill Burgess leaned over the rail, giddy with excitement, and called out, "You've got it now, Gertie, you've got it now!" As she swam to within a few hundred yards of the beach, Burgess, her father, and a crew member lowered a rowboat into the water and rowed ashore ahead of her. They wanted to make sure no one touched her until she was absolutely free of the water.

Trudy increased her pace and swam as if she were competing in a race of only a few hundred meters, trying not to think, just focusing on the next stroke and the next breath.

All of a sudden her hand touched the bottom. She floated to a stop and stood in the thigh-deep water as small waves pushed her toward shore. She took a few unsteady steps and then walked confidently out of the shallows. As her father approached her with a robe, she put up her hand. "Stay back, Pop, stay back," she called, not taking any chances. Then she stepped onto the sand, and the sea reached for her and then rushed back.

She was across. Fourteen hours and thirty-one minutes after entering the water in France, Trudy Ederle stepped onto the shore at Kingsdown Beach in England, only the sixth person, and first woman, ever to swim the Channel. Her time was nearly two hours faster than that of the male record holder's.

"So," she said to her father as he wrapped her in the robe, "do I get that red roadster?" Her father just laughed. She would get that car, but that wasn't as important as the gift Trudy had just given to every woman in the world. She had proven that women could compete in athletics—and she had shown that in some cases they were even better than men.

Today, on athletic fields, at swimming pools, and in gymnasiums around the world, wherever women compete in sports, people still feel the ripples from Trudy's big splash.

LOUISE STOKES AND TIDYE PICKETT

America's first two African American female Olympians, Louise Stokes (top right) and Tidye Pickett (third from right, bottom), pose with their teammates on the U.S. women's track team before traveling to Germany for the 1936 Olympic Games.

THE REAL WINNERS

Sometimes a person becomes a pioneer by breaking a record or winning a race. But sometimes pioneers break barriers simply by refusing to quit. They are the real winners.

That is what Louise Stokes and Tidye (pronounced "Teddy") Pickett did. No matter how unfairly they were treated, they refused to quit. Their perseverance and courage made it possible for other girls to compete.

In the wake of Trudy Ederle's successful swim across the English Channel, more women were allowed access to athletics. At the 1928 Olympic Games, women were allowed to compete in track and field for the first time, competing in the 100- and 800-meter individual sprint races, the 4x100-meter relay, the high jump, and the discus.

Unfortunately, some women at the 1928 Games were not adequately prepared to run. In the 800-meter, several competitors dropped out before finishing, and others collapsed at the end of the race. Some observers saw these failures as evidence that women were not capable of running more than a few yards, and believed that, as one critic put it, running was "dangerous to feminine nature." Some even tried to convince the International Olympic Committee (IOC) to drop women's track and field altogether.

The IOC almost did just that. But one year before the 1932 games, they decided to allow women to continue to compete in track and field, although the 800-meter run was dropped.

After the 1928 Olympics, track clubs for girls and young women popped up all over the United States. Once women started running, they could not be stopped.

Louise Stokes, a young African American woman from Massachusetts, loved to run. The granddaughter of slaves, Louise was the oldest of six children born to William Stokes, a gardener, and his wife, Mary, a housekeeper. The Stokeses were part of a small but vibrant African American community in the town of Malden, a suburb of Boston.

In the ninth grade Louise attended Beebe Junior High

School and played on the girls' basketball team. Louise loved running up and down the court with her teammates. In fact, Louise ran whenever she could. Years later her friends could still remember seeing her run through the streets of Malden when she went to visit her friends. She enjoyed going as fast as her legs could carry her, and she even enjoyed the exhausted way she felt after running, when her whole body seemed to vibrate with life.

One day in 1930 one of Louise's teammates on the basketball team, Kathryn Robley, told Louise she had joined a group called the Onteora Track Club. A local postal worker, William Quain, who also served as Malden's parks commissioner, had started the club to give local girls an opportunity to run and to train for other track events.

Louise contacted Quain and he invited her to join the team. Although Quain and most of the girls on the club were white, Quain was not prejudiced against African Americans. But when Louise showed up for her first practice, she was surprised that instead of going to a local park, Quain brought the girls to a set of railroad tracks that serviced a local commuter train. Those train tracks provided the "track" for the Onteora Track Club. The high school track was reserved for the use of the boys' track team and was not available to Quain and his club. He had considered having the girls practice at one of Malden's parks, but there was not enough flat ground to run sprints of more than a few dozen yards. The only available stretch of flat ground nearby was the wide cinder and gravel path on the right of way between two sets of train tracks that ran between Malden and the nearby town of Saugus.

Louise and the other members of the team turned out for practice every day after school. Taking special care not to cross the tracks when a train was approaching, Quain led them on long training runs back and forth beside the tracks. He also measured off various distances and had them run sprints, both against each other and against the stopwatch he wore around his neck. He taught the girls how to use a "sprinter's crouch" at the start of a run and how to use their arms to help drive their legs forward. He built makeshift hurdles for the girls who wanted to try to run that event and taught them how to clear the barriers without breaking stride. He also gave instruction in the standing broad jump and the high jump.

Running along the railroad tracks was the highlight of Louise's day. She did not mind when the occasional stumble in the gravel left her knees and elbows skinned and bloody. As they ran, Louise and her teammates found it easy to imagine that they were running on a track in a big stadium. In Louise's imagination, the sound of distant car traffic and passing trains became the roar of the crowd. She even carried a big watch of her own to keep track of her times.

The girls of the Onteora Track Club became so familiar to rail commuters that as the trains raced past, the passengers would wave and call out words of encouragement. Sometimes neighborhood children would try to keep up with Louise. Many years later, one man recalled that it had been impossible. As the exhausted youngsters fell behind, Louise just kept going. "She would be out of sight in about a minute," he said. Louise was confident in her ability and told the children, "Someday, I'll be the best."

Quain soon realized that although all the girls on the team were talented and worked hard, Louise was special. She was easily the fastest member of the club, and one of the hardest workers. As one of the club members later recalled, Louise was "Mr. Quain's number one on the track. It was obvious right away that she was our best runner."

Each fall the mayor of Boston, James Michael Curley, sponsored a big track meet. In 1931, the meet was held at Fens Stadium in a Boston park. Athletes from all over the Boston area were invited to compete. Quain's club had already competed in a few unofficial meets against some other local women's track teams, and Louise and some of her teammates had done well.

Quain entered Louise and her teammates in Mayor Curley's track meet. When they arrived at the stadium, they were stunned. Hundreds of athletes were waiting to compete, and the grandstand was packed with thousands of fans. Reporters from Boston's biggest newspapers scurried around, interviewing coaches and athletes.

Louise and her teammates could not believe how many other young girls were racing. Instead of holding one race in each event, officials had to hold several races, known as heats. The top finishers in each heat then competed, until the very best runners faced off against each other in the finals.

For Louise, the day went by in a blur. She competed in three events—the 100-yard dash, the 50-yard dash, and the standing broad jump. It seemed that as soon as she raced in one heat, she had to run in another or jump in the broad jump. She made the finals in all three events, finishing third in the broad jump and second in the 50-yard dash.

But she saved her best performance for the 100-yard dash. Despite being exhausted from running several races already, Louise got off to a quick start and with each stride began to pull away from the other runners. This time the roar of the crowd was real. She was the first runner to break the tape. But Louise did more than just win. She also set a New England record, winning the race in 12.6 seconds. No other girl in the region, of any age, had ever run so fast. At the end of the meet, Louise was awarded a big bronze trophy, the Curley Cup, for being the outstanding performer at the meet. News of Louise's accomplishment spread fast, and overnight she was recognized as one of the best female track athletes in the country. Newspapers started referring to her as the Malden Meteor. Quain began to believe that Louise was good enough to compete in the Olympics.

Halfway across the country, in a Chicago neighborhood known as Englewood, another young African American woman was also making a name for herself as a track athlete. The daughter of Sarah and Louis Pickett, who worked for the International Harvester Company, Theodora Ann Pickett, known to everyone by her nickname, Tidye, loved sports and played basketball for the team at Englewood High School. Like her older brother Charles, Tidye was a terrific student. She served as the Englewood correspondent for the *Chicago Defender*, one of the biggest African

American newspapers in the country. Soon, however, instead of Tidye writing for the *Defender*, the *Defender* would be writing about her.

Tidye's family lived across the street from Washington Park in Chicago. The *Chicago Daily News* sometimes held picnics at the park and sponsored races for local boys and girls. Every time they did, Tidye would go home with the winning prize.

One day, Tidye was with some friends at a nearby school playground when Pearl Greene, director of the girls' athletic program for the Chicago Board of Education Playground Programs, saw Tidye race past. She did a double take. She had never seen a young girl run so quickly. She called out to Tidye and persuaded her to join a team. Tidye agreed and joined the Chicago Park District's South Park track team. Soon coaches were teaching Tidye how to sprint and run and jump, just as William Quain was doing for Louise. And like Louise, Tidye also began to compete in track meets.

At one meet, held indoors at a Chicago armory, another, older track star named John Brooks watched Tidye run. Her long stride, her speed, and her look of determination made her stand out. Brooks, a member of the track team at the University of Chicago and one of the best long jumpers in the country, was impressed. He sought out Tidye's parents and asked if he could train their daughter. They agreed. Brooks supplied Tidye with proper track shoes and clothing and soon began teaching her the finer points of sprinting, running the hurdles, and executing the high jump. Brooks was hoping to compete in the 1932 Summer Olympics, to be held in Los Angeles, and he believed that Tidye might make the women's team. As Tidye later recalled, when Brooks began to train her, "That was it—I'm gone."

Neither Louise nor Tidye was aware of just how difficult it would be to make the Olympic team. Although African American men had already proved they belonged on the U.S. team—some had even won medals—African American women had not. To make the team, athletes had to qualify at the Olympic trials. But it was impossible to just walk up and ask to compete. Potential team members had to be invited.

Both Louise and Tidye soon became familiar to track fans in their hometowns. Nearly every time they competed, they came away with a victory. Louise was particularly successful.

On the last day of December in 1931, at an indoor meet sponsored by the Young Men's Hebrew Association in

Boston, Louise competed in the standing broad jump, a track event rarely held today. She took a deep breath and stood with her toes just behind the starting line, swinging her arms back and forth in unison and bobbing up and down. Then she went into a deep crouch and exploded up and out, throwing her arms ahead of herself. Louise stretched out her legs as she landed, her heels making a mark on the track as she landed. As she watched, meet officials carefully measured the distance she had jumped, and then measured it again and again.

They were dumbfounded. Louise had jumped eight feet, five and three quarter inches—a women's world record! The unknown girl from Malden was now the subject of headlines. Her spectacular performance earned her invitations to a number of meets over the next few months. She won the Curley Cup for the second year in a row, and she won the New England Amateur Athletic Union (AAU) title in the 100-yard dash. She was clearly one of the best all-around women's track stars in the country. Her record performances earned her an invitation to the Olympic trials at Northwestern University in Evanston, Illinois.

Meanwhile, in Chicago, Tidye Pickett was enjoying similar success in track meets sponsored by the Chicago Parks Department. Like Louise, she was invited to compete in the Olympic trials. She and Louise were the first African American women invited to the trials. To make the team, they would have to prove themselves in competitions against dozens of young women from all over the country.

Before the tryouts began, the big story was the appearance of a young woman from Texas, Babe Didrikson, one of the best all-around female athletes in the world. The brash young Texan seemed to excel at every sport she tried, and newspaper reporters loved writing about her. Because of Didrikson, the Olympic trials received a great deal of attention.

Many of the young women, like Didrikson, were accompanied to the trials by their own coaches and trainers. The personal coaches waited on their athletes and made it easy for them to concentrate on competing. One sprinter was even carried back and forth to the track by her coach so she would stay rested! If anything went wrong, the coaches went running to members of the American Olympic Committee (AOC) to complain.

Neither Louise nor Tidye was fortunate enough to have her own coach at the trials. The women were on their own. Conditions were tough. It was very humid, and temperatures hovered near one hundred degrees during the meet. To stay cool, the young women sat on big blocks of ice between events. There would be several heats for each event; the finals would determine who made the team.

Both Louise and Tidye were entered in the 100-meter run—the broad jump was not an Olympic event. American Olympic officials planned to select a total of six sprinters based on the results of the trials. Some would compete in the 100-meter individual race, and some in the 400-meter relay, a race in which four women each run one hundred meters.

Six to eight young women from around the country competed in seven heats. The top two finishers in each heat ran in two semifinal events, and the top three in each semifinal made the finals. All the women who made the finals were assured of spots on the Olympic team. The fastest runners would compete in the individual sprint at the Olympics and the others in the relay. At least, that was what everyone was told before the competition began.

Louise and Tidye ran fast but smart, making sure they qualified for the finals, yet conserving their energy for the semifinals. Each girl finished second in her first heat, and in the top three in the semifinals, becoming one of six girls to earn a place in the finals—and a spot on the Olympic team!

At least, they *thought* they had made the team. But when Louise and Tidye took their places at the start of the finals, they noticed that there were not six runners lined up to race, but seven.

In one of the earlier heats, one runner, Ethel Harrington, had misjudged the finish line, stopped running, and missed qualifying. But Ethel's coach was at the meet, and after the race he complained and convinced Olympic officials to allow her to compete in the finals anyway. Since she had only run in a single heat, she was much fresher than Louise or Tidye. And now, with seven women in the finals, it appeared that whoever finished last would be left off the team. Had the other women known that, they might have raced differently in the semifinals to save some energy for the next race. Now it was too late.

When the starter's gun went off, everyone started sprinting. Although a few of the women had finished the race in under twelve seconds earlier in the day, by now everyone was exhausted and running much slower.

When Louise lunged for the tape at the finish line, it fluttered to the ground an instant before she reached it. She had not won, but she knew she had been very close to first place. In fact, she had tied for third place. But Tidye Pickett did not run quite so well. Although she tried her best, she finished last, in seventh place.

When the results were announced, Tidye was crushed. She felt that it had been unfair to add another woman to the final even though she had failed to qualify for it. But there was nothing Tidye could do. Unlike some other women, she did not have a coach there to argue her case.

Fortunately, George T. Donohue, one of the judges of the race, also thought that the addition of a seventh runner had been unfair. He argued that by reaching the finals, Tidye had already earned a spot on the team. Reluctantly, AOC officials agreed. As the *Chicago Defender* noted later, "Mr. Donohue stepped up and fought for Tidye's place in the finals.... Mr. Donohue, white, is to be congratulated for his fairness." Now Tidye joined Louise as an official member of the team.

With the Olympics scheduled to begin in only a few days, soon after the meet the entire team boarded a train for Los Angeles. The women had their own rail car, and a big banner reading THE U.S. OLYMPIC TEAM hung over the side. They were all proud and happy, and enjoyed one another's company.

Well, most of them did. Babe Didrikson had been the big star of the trials, and her teammates thought her success had gone to her head. Some of the women thought she was a braggart and disliked her. And Didrikson, in turn, did not like some of her teammates. Louise and Tidye felt that Didrikson particularly did not like them. As Louise's sister Emily later admitted to a reporter, "Louise told us it was racial problems....Didrikson never liked her and Tidye Pickett."

When they reached Denver, the train stopped to give the women a chance to rest and work out before continuing to Los Angeles. They were taken to one of the best hotels in Denver, the opulent Brown Palace. But Louise and Tidye would soon learn that not all team members were treated the same. When they tried to enter the hotel, they were stopped by a hotel employee. The hotel was segregated, meaning that African Americans were not allowed to use the same facilities as white guests. Louise and Tidye were not even allowed to enter the hotel through the main entrance. They were told to use the back.

The other women on the team did not think that was fair, and many followed Louise and Tidye around to the back entrance. The women appreciated the gesture of support, but that did not end their trouble at the hotel.

While Babe Didrikson and their other teammates each enjoyed private rooms, Louise and Tidye shared a small, spare room that was usually occupied by African Americans who worked at the hotel. And while their teammates attended an elegant banquet reception in the hotel ballroom, Tidye and Louise were not even invited — African Americans were only allowed in the ballroom if they were working as waiters or other hotel staff. As Tidye Pickett later recalled, "Louise and I shared a room in the attic and ate our dinners upstairs on trays." The two young women could not help wondering whether they were truly welcome on the team.

Fortunately, when they arrived in Los Angeles, they were no longer segregated from the other Olympic athletes — at least, not by race. The 1932 Olympic Games were the first that featured an athletes' village, a place where participants from all over the world stayed together and got to know one another.

But a few athletes stayed elsewhere. American Olympic officials did not think it was appropriate for American female athletes to stay in a facility near male athletes, so the entire U.S. women's Olympic team, including Louise and Tidye, stayed at the Chapman Park Hotel. Apart from that, however, before the competition began, they were all treated the same. The team participated in all the events that surrounded the games, such as a visit to the Fox movie studio. During their visit, movie star Janet Gaynor handed out small gifts — Louise received a compact.

The opening ceremony in the Los Angeles Coliseum was spectacular, and Louise and Tidye, dressed like their teammates in long white skirts, white blouses, red and blue vests, and wide-brimmed white hats, proudly paraded around the track as nearly one hundred thousand fans roared and cheered. Unfortunately, the opening and the closing ceremonies would be the only time Tidye and Louise would appear on the track.

Although they were enjoying their sightseeing, the women were in Los Angeles to run. Once again, however, they met a barrier to their participation. Evelyn Furtsch, who had failed to qualify in Evanston when she stumbled and fell, was added to the team. Now there were eight sprinters on the team, with room for only six to compete on the track.

All eight women, including Louise and Tidye, continued to train for both the individual sprints and the relays.

But when it was time to compete, team coach Lawson Robertson selected neither Tidye nor Louise. Neither young woman was even given an explanation.

One member of the team, Wilhelmina von Bremen, who had won the 100-meter trials in Illinois, competed in both the 100-meter individual race and the relay. Two other women competed in the individual race, and three others, including Evelyn Furtsch and Ethel Harrington—the two women who had originally failed to qualify—and Mary Carew, who had tied Louise in the finals, were all selected to run in the relay.

Louise and Tidye watched and cheered as Wilhelmina von Bremen won a bronze medal in the 100-meter, losing to Stella Walsh of Poland, and their teammates set a world record in the 400-meter relay to win a gold medal.

Back in Chicago and Malden, Louise's and Tidye's friends and families looked for their names in the local newspapers the day after the competitions. They could not understand why they did not see Louise and Tidye listed. They had no idea what had happened until the young women wrote home and brief stories appeared in the local African American newspapers saying that neither one had been allowed to compete.

No one outside the African American press made an issue out of the snub, and even the newspapers used restraint. Everyone in the African American community knew that if they complained too loudly, they might make it even more difficult for an African American woman to compete in the Olympics in the future.

Louise and Tidye were crushed, but as Louise later explained, they didn't complain either, knowing that it was fruitless to do so. "Maybe if I had my manager [William Quain] at the Olympics, things would have been different," she told a reporter many years later. "But I was a mere child...just a cute girl that didn't know anything."

The white women on the team barely noticed that their African American teammates had not been allowed to race. It was not their fault, and as one said later, "We were eighteen years old. We never questioned the authority of the coaches." But in his official report, team manager Fred Steers suggested that American Olympic officials had interfered. He complained, "I further recommend that all matters pertaining to the team be transacted and carried on through the Manager only. This was not done in many cases and as a result, considerable confusion was caused."

Both young women returned to their hometowns. Instead of becoming bitter and allowing the incident to deter them, each became more determined than ever to compete and earn a place on the 1936 Olympic team.

Over the next four years, both women won race after race. Louise won the Curley Cup again in 1933, and later that year, in a race in Chicago, she defeated two of her white Olympic teammates to win the AAU 100-meter championship. Louise even dropped out of high school to focus on running, working as a domestic to help support her family. By the time of the tryouts for the 1936 Olympics, Louise was the national 50-yard champion and the New England AAU champ in the 100-yard, the 200-meter, the 220-yard, the broad jump, and the high jump. Tidye Pickett set a world record in the 40-yard dash and won a national title in the 50-yard hurdles. At the Olympic trials she decided to concentrate on making the team in the 80-meter high hurdles, an event that would be held for the first time at the 1936 Olympics in Berlin, Germany.

At the trials in Providence, Rhode Island, both women earned places on the team for the second Olympics in a row. This time, however, it was Louise who needed the help of the judges. After winning her heat in the 100-meter dash in both the preliminaries and the semifinals, she was leading the field in the finals when she glanced over her shoulder, broke stride, and nearly stumbled. She finished fifth, yet Olympic officials still named her to the team. Tidye earned her spot by finishing third in the finals of the 80-meter hurdles.

But there was one more hurdle for each of the two young women. Although the expenses for all the competitors in the 1932 Olympics had been paid by the American Olympic Committee, in 1936, with the nation deep in an economic depression, the AOC was broke. They made a new rule, a "quota system" that required each American team member to raise at least five hundred dollars to pay for the cost of traveling to Berlin. If an athlete failed to raise the funds, he or she would be removed from the team.

For some athletes, many of whom came from wealthy families or big track clubs and other well-established athletic organizations, raising five hundred dollars was not very difficult. But for Tidye and Louise, it might as well have been five million. Neither came from a wealthy family.

Louise was fortunate: the mayor of Malden came to her rescue and raised the money himself. Tidye, however, was not so lucky. She had failed to raise her quota and was about to be left behind. Three other members of the team had a similar problem. But at the last minute, the AOC decided to fund the four athletes, including Tidye. "They must have thought I was good," she said later. "They were depending on me to win." Still, as both young women would soon learn, the quota system created another set of problems. Some athletes and their sponsors who had raised more than five hundred dollars believed they should receive special treatment.

Even before the U.S. team arrived in Berlin, their participation in the Games was controversial. Germany was controlled by Adolf Hitler and the Nazi party, and by 1936 it was becoming clear the Nazis considered Jewish people and members of other ethnic groups to be subhuman. The Nazis believed that Germans were "the master race" and hoped to prove it at the Olympics. Some nations boycotted the games. The makeup of the American Olympic team, which not only included Jews, but also a number of African Americans like Louise, Tidye, and male track star Jesse Owens, was offensive to the Nazis, who believed that African Americans, like Jews, were subhuman.

But the African Americans on the men's track team proved that the Nazis were wrong. They dominated nearly every event in which they competed. Jesse Owens was the big star, winning gold medals in the 100-meter dash, the 400-meter dash, and the long jump.

Owens was originally not supposed to run in the 400-meter relay. But with a chance to win a fourth gold medal, he and another African American, Ralph Metcalfe, were added to the team.

At least that was what the AOC said. The two runners Owens and Metcalfe replaced were Sam Stoller and Marty Glickman, two Jewish Americans. Many people thought they had been dropped from the event because American officials thought Adolf Hitler would be offended if they ran in the relay. Nevertheless, on August 4, Owens and the relay team still won the gold medal.

On August 5, Tidye Pickett became the first African American woman to compete in the Olympics when she raced in a preliminary heat in the 80-meter hurdles. She finished third, well enough to make the semifinals. If she finished third or better in the semis, she would run in the finals and have a chance to win a medal.

Tidye started the semifinal race on the outside of the track, in the sixth position. In the first heat she had paced herself, saving her energy. Now she knew she had to run as fast as possible. When the starter's gun went off, Tidye exploded from the blocks. Although she knew she was the first African American woman to run at the Olympics, she was not thinking about that as she ran. She was just trying to lift her lead leg over each hurdle as quickly as possible.

That might have been the problem—she tried to go too fast. After clearing several hurdles cleanly, she hit one with her back foot. Unlike the hurdles she was accustomed to using in the United States, which toppled over easily and allowed runners to continue to race, the hurdles in Germany were made of heavy steel. It tripped her up.

Tidye went sprawling onto the track, hurting her ankle and bruising her shoulder. As she tumbled to the cinders, her dream of an Olympic medal slipped away. She was disappointed, but she knew she had tried her best. This time, at least, she had been allowed to run.

Although there had been some speculation before the games that Pickett might also run in the 400-meter relay, now that was impossible. It was time for Louise to get her chance.

When Louise awoke on August 9, she dressed and traveled with her teammates to the stadium, prepared to run. But when it came time for the 400-meter race, as Louise said later, she found "other runners in our places." She recalled that she "just had to stand there, and I felt terrible. I really should have said something after it was done, but what could you do? The worst part of it all is that they never said a word about it."

Some people believed that Louise had been removed from the team and replaced by a white runner to make up for the removal of the two white Jewish runners from the men's 400-meter team. Others believed that a sponsor of one of the white members of the women's team who had contributed more money under the "quota system" than Louise had gotten Louise bumped.

Louise herself never learned the real reason she was not allowed to run, although once again, in the final report of the games, team manager Fred Steers may have provided a clue. He complained that the quota system "led to considerable embarrassment to the coach of our group, particularly in the selection of a relay team." Nevertheless, the U.S. women won a gold medal in the 400-meter relay when the German team, leading by nine meters at the beginning of the final lap, dropped the baton.

Louise Stokes and Tidye Pickett returned to America, their Olympic dreams over. Both were saddened by the events of the Games, but neither woman allowed what happened to affect the rest of their lives.

Tidye Pickett married, had two children and adopted another, and worked her way through college. She eventually earned a master's degree from Northern Illinois University, becoming a teacher and then an elementary school principal. When she retired in 1980, an elementary school in Chicago was named after her.

Although she was disappointed that she hadn't been allowed to run in 1932 and saddened by the prejudice she faced, she remained philosophical. "I knew I was better than some of them," she once said. "It was politics. Politics and sports. Sports and politics, they've always gone together." She passed away in 1986.

When Louise Stokes returned home to Malden after the 1936 Olympics, she was given a big welcome-home party and parade by her hometown. But soon after her return, as her sister recalled, "She politely stopped running." She married, had a son, and worked for the Commonwealth of Massachusetts before retiring in 1975, three years before passing away.

At least Tidye Pickett had gotten a chance to run. Louise never had, and it weighed heavily upon her. Her sister described her as a "very friendly person" who thought "everyone was wonderful, until she found out they weren't.

"After she returned from Germany she never talked about it much. You'd have to sit down and pull the information out of her. We knew more about what happened in California than in Germany."

Yet Louise never asked why she had not been allowed to compete. "She was not that kind of person," said her sister. "She was just a very nice, quiet person, humble, and she stayed to herself. She had a lot of fun with Tidye. They had a very good time...but she was very disappointed they didn't compete."

Still, in their own way, Louise and Tidye did compete— and they won something more valuable than any Olympic medal. By their example as pioneers in women's sports, they won the biggest victory of all—our everlasting admiration and respect.

Because of World War II, the Olympics were not held in either 1940 or 1944. When the Games resumed in 1948, only one American woman earned a medal, a gold medal in the high jump.

That gold medal was won by Alice Coachman, an African American.

Julie Krone in her jockey silks and protective helmet, ready to race.

RACING AHEAD

WHEN JULIE KRONE WAS GROWING UP in rural Michigan, she did not just like horses — she *loved* horses!

As far back as Julie can remember, she has always been around horses. Her father, Don, taught art and photography in high school and college, but her mother, Judi, raised show horses, and when Julie was old enough, both mother and daughter competed in equestrian events. Julie and her older brother, Donnie, were brought into the barn when they were still infants. Julie grew up around horses, and though the animals towered over her, she was never afraid.

Although Julie's mother sometimes held her in her lap when she rode, Julie took her first ride alone by accident. When she was only two years old, her mother put a beautiful palomino up for sale. A buyer came by, and Judi wanted to demonstrate that the horse was gentle and good-natured. She picked up two-year-old Julie and plopped her on the horse.

The palomino immediately cantered across the riding ring with Julie on her back. As her mother watched in amazement, little Julie reached out, grabbed the reins, and gave them a gentle tug to one side, as if she had been riding horses since the day she was born. The horse stopped, turned around, and trotted right back to Julie's mother!

After that, it was almost impossible to keep Julie off a horse, or any other animal. Julie's dog, Trigger, even let her climb on his back and ride him around the yard. Julie's father once joked that "she made a horse out of everything. If she couldn't find a racehorse, she'd jump on our backs and make racehorses out of us."

When Julie was five, her mother got a young colt named Ibn. Together, Julie and her mother raised and trained the colt. Every morning, no matter how cold it was, Julie had to trudge out to the barn, feed and water Ibn, and clean out his stall. In the afternoon when she came home from school, she had to spend hours working with the horse under her mother's supervision. She learned to introduce Ibn to a bridle and a saddle and ever so gently earned Ibn's trust until he allowed her to ride him. Ibn and Julie became best friends. She was devastated when Ibn got loose one night and was struck and killed by a car.

A short time later, the family moved to a small farm and was able to keep even more animals. They had a cat named Ben, a Saint Bernard named Gretta, a Great Dane named Arrow, and all sorts of farm animals, including Filly, who was half Arabian horse and half Shetland pony.

It was Julie's responsibility to care for Filly, but this horse wasn't like Ibn. While Ibn had been easy to train and care for, Filly was stubborn. Nevertheless, every day when Julie got out of school, she ran from the bus to the barn to begin working with her pony.

Sometimes Filly would run away when Julie approached her, or would lie on her back and kick her legs in the air when Julie tried to put a saddle on her. When Julie did manage to mount her, Filly sometimes tried to buck her off or would run off before Julie was settled into the saddle.

Every day was an adventure with Filly, but Julie did not give up on her. Julie was even more stubborn than her pony, and over time the animal grew to trust her. In fact, Julie learned more about horses from a difficult horse like Filly than she would have from a calmer animal. She began to understand that though she was training Filly, Filly was also training her. As a result, Julie not only learned a great deal about horses, but also became a better rider and a more patient person.

Julie loved taking Filly for long rides along the roads and trails near her home. Although some of the neighbors worried that young Julie would get hurt, her parents trusted her. Eventually, Filly even allowed Julie to do tricks, such as standing on Filly's back without holding on as the horse galloped around.

Whenever Julie wasn't riding horses, she was thinking about riding horses. She wrote poems about horses and painted pictures of horses. She even put an old saddle on top of a trunk in her room, then tied some reins to her bed, sat in the saddle, and pretended she was riding. Daydreaming about horses, Julie could lose herself for hours.

Unfortunately, she could not daydream all the time. At school, Julie found it hard to concentrate, and she struggled with schoolwork. Sometimes when she looked at a page in a book or a worksheet of math problems, the letters and numbers seemed all jumbled up and she could not figure out the words or come up with the answers. As a result, Julie was easily frustrated and spent most of her time in class fidgeting. All she wanted to do was stay home and spend time with her animals.

But none of her problems at school were her fault. She did not know it at the time, but years later, when Julie was an adult, she was told she had both dyslexia, a learning disorder that can make it difficult to read and spell, and dyscalculia, a similar disorder that can make doing math problems difficult. She also had attention deficit disorder, which was why she found it almost impossible to sit still and concentrate. Julie knew she was not stupid, but sometimes it seemed that the only ones who knew that were her family — and her pony, Filly.

When Julie began high school, her frustrations only grew. All her friends were growing up, but Julie remained small and looked much younger than they did. She was a young woman but was often treated like a little kid. There was trouble at home, too. Her parents decided to divorce, and her father and brother moved out of the house. Her mother got a job at night working as a bartender.

Julie was miserable. She began acting out in school. Her life was at a crossroads. She had no interest in anything — except horses.

Then, in 1978, when Julie was fourteen years old, she found her purpose.

Horses known as thoroughbreds are the fastest horses in the world. People have ridden and raced thoroughbreds for hundreds of years. Horseracing became so popular among English nobility that it was known as the sport of kings. Although thoroughbreds were once raced over distances of several miles, today most thoroughbred races are between three-quarters of a mile and a mile and a half.

In the United States the biggest and most lucrative horse races — the Kentucky Derby, the Preakness, and the Belmont Stakes—are known collectively as the Triple Crown. These races feature the fastest three-year old horses in the world. They are like the World Series or Super Bowl of horse racing. Only eleven horses have ever managed to win all three races in one year and earn the Triple Crown.

In 1978, Julie and her mother watched on television as a jockey named Steve Cauthen, riding a beautiful horse named Affirmed, won the Kentucky Derby. A few weeks later, they also won the Preakness. That got Julie's attention, and not just because Affirmed was a beautiful horse. Steve Cauthen was only eighteen years old, only a few years older than Julie, yet he was already one of the best jockeys in the world.

Julie and her mother were glued to their television when it was time to watch Cauthen and Affirmed race in the Belmont Stakes and try to win the Triple Crown. From the moment the horse broke from the starting gate, Julie was mesmerized. With each stride, a dream began to take shape in Julie's mind.

As Cauthen and Affirmed thundered across the finish line to win the Belmont and the Triple Crown, it finally dawned on Julie what she wanted to do with her life.

"Mom," she said, "I'm going to be a jockey.... Someday that's gonna be me out there!" Julie Krone, a young woman, wanted to crash the sport of kings.

Julie did not yet realize it, but in the history of thoroughbred racing, there had been only a handful of female jockeys. In fact, there had been none at all until 1969, when pioneers Kathy Kusner, Diane Crump, Barbara Jo Rubin, and Tuesdee Testa were the first female jockeys to break the barrier. In 1978, female jockeys were still rare and faced a great deal of resistance from male jockeys, trainers, and horse owners. Many did not think women were strong enough or tough enough to race.

Julie had no idea how hard it would be for her to fulfill her dream. In racing terms, her dream was a long shot. The odds were against her.

Even though Julie's mother knew that female jockeys were rare, she did nothing to discourage her daughter. A few days after the Belmont, Julie read a biography of Cauthen. She became even more convinced that she wanted to be a jockey. She plastered the walls of her room with pictures of jockeys, and she learned all she could about jockeys and the sport of horseracing.

There is no such thing as jockey school. The only way to become a jockey is by working at a racetrack and learning the profession from the ground up.

That could have been a problem for Julie. There were no thoroughbred racetracks near her home in Michigan. But over the summer, she and her mother talked about her dream. Her mother told her that if she really wanted to become a jockey, she would have to work for it. Together they decided that during spring break, they would travel to Churchill Downs in Louisville, Kentucky, and try to line up a job at the track for Julie the following summer.

All fall and winter, Julie dreamed about racing. When she was riding Filly or another horse around the farm, she pretended she was riding down the backstretch, fighting for the lead. She even tried to ride like a jockey, cutting the stirrups on her saddle short to mimic a jockey's saddle and lift her body up and forward. Jockeys do not sit on a horse's back as much as they crouch over its shoulders to help press the horse ahead.

April finally came, and Julie and her mom made the long drive to Kentucky. But since Julie's parents had divorced, money was tight. They could only afford to stay in Kentucky three days. If they were going to stay longer, they each had to find a job.

When they arrived at Churchill Downs, they only spent a few moments looking at the grand twin spires of the famous grandstand. Then they went straight to the barn and started asking horse trainers if they needed any help.

They got lucky. Each was hired to work a few days as a hot walker, a person who walks a horse after exercise to help it cool down safely. They were able to stay for an entire week. By the time they had to return to Michigan, trainer Clarence Pictou had agreed to give Julie a job the following summer.

The rest of the spring went by in a flash. In June, Julie returned to Kentucky and went to work for Clarence for fifty dollars a week while she lived with him and his wife.

She did anything she was asked, from mucking stalls to bathing horses, learning everything there was to know about taking care of thoroughbreds. She told Clarence, a former jockey himself, that she wanted to be a jockey and asked over and over again, "When can I ride?"

Clarence was impressed with Julie's work ethic and her knowledge of horses and realized that her small size made her dream possible. The less a jockey weighs, the faster a horse can run, so few jockeys weigh more than 110 pounds or so. Julie was just under five feet tall and weighed less than one hundred pounds, so Clarence finally relented and allowed Julie to begin exercising his horses on the track at Churchill Downs.

The first few times she galloped down the track on the back of a prize thoroughbred that weighed almost two thousand pounds, Julie could hardly believe it. The stands went by in a blur and she imagined she could hear the roar of the crowd over the thundering hooves of her horse. But she was not intimidated. She loved every part of it, from the way the horse smelled to the feel of the wind in her face and the ache in her arms and her back after a long day riding.

Summer went by quickly, and Julie had to return to Michigan — and high school. Sitting in class again was not nearly as exciting as working at the track, but she somehow made it through another year. The next summer she went to live with one of her mother's friends who owned and raced quarter horses. Quarter horses are a bit smaller than thoroughbreds, and as the name suggests, they race short sprints of a quarter of a mile. Still, it takes a great deal of skill to ride them.

Julie rode in about sixty races that summer, gaining experience and confidence. She even managed to win a few times!

But at the end of the summer, once again, Julie had to return to school. And once again, she was not very happy. All she wanted to do was ride.

It was a difficult decision, but in December, Julie's mother allowed her to quit school and go to live with her grandparents in Tampa, Florida. There was a track nearby, and Julie planned to get a job there.

As soon as she had moved to Tampa, Julie snuck onto the Tampa Bay Downs track before it was open so she could look for a job. She happened to meet trainer Jerry Pace. She looked up at him and said boldly, "I'm gonna be a jockey." Pace laughed, but he could tell that Julie was determined. He allowed Julie to ride one of his horses and was impressed by her knowledge and poise. He took on an apprentice jockey every year and decided to take a chance on Julie. Within a week she had earned her jockey's license, which showed she knew how to ride safely. Now all she needed was a chance to ride in a race.

One month later, on January 30, 1981, she got that chance. She finished second in her first race. Two weeks later, on February 12, she won for the first time, on a horse named Lord Farkle. But just because Julie had won a race, that did not mean she knew everything about riding horses.

Every time she got on a horse, she learned something new. Jerry Pace worked with her on her technique, and Julie studied other jockeys. She also had to get to know every horse she was supposed to ride so she knew how to treat it during training or in a race. Some horses liked to be pushed. Others did not. Some ran only after being whipped, while others sulked when struck. Some horses liked to bolt ahead and some liked to run from behind, or stay along the rail, or stay wide and out of traffic. Every time Julie took a horse onto the track, she had to be aware of a thousand little things that could make the difference between winning and losing.

She also had to learn about strategy. To win, a jockey has to do more than get his or her horse to run. He or she has to anticipate what other jockeys are planning to do. During a race, jockeys maneuver their horses like chess pieces, boxing other horses in, forcing some to run wide, and trying to stay in front. At the same time, jockeys also have to learn to ride safely, making sure that the horses do not collide or stumble. If a horse tumbles and falls during a race, both the jockey and the horse can be seriously hurt or even killed.

Julie also had to learn to get along with the other jockeys. Although the jockeys shared the same facilities at the track, they were all in competition, not only on the track but also in the barns, where jockeys had to convince trainers to hire them.

As the only female jockey at the Tampa track, Julie often felt left out. Although some jockeys were nice to her, others thought she did not belong there and were either rude or acted as if she did not exist.

But all her years of experience quickly paid off. In her first forty-eight rides she placed in the top three twenty-three times, winning nine races. Chick Lang, a jockey agent, told Julie he could get her races at bigger tracks up north and convinced her to move to Maryland.

A jockey moving to the larger tracks is like a baseball player going from the minor leagues to the majors. The prize money is better, the horses are faster, and the jockeys are tougher and more experienced. But Julie started winning immediately, and the other jockeys soon realized that she was good. Instead of ignoring her, they considered Julie a threat.

Over the next several years, Julie gained experience and racked up one win after another at racetracks in Maryland, New Jersey, and elsewhere. She had to fight for every victory. She knew that if she let the other jockeys push her around, she would never gain their respect, no matter how many races she won.

On one occasion, as she raced toward the finish line, another jockey, perhaps jealous of Julie's success, smacked Julie's horse with his whip. It was a dangerous and illegal act. Although Julie maintained control of her horse, the move could have caused him to stumble or bump into another horse. Julie, another jockey, or a horse might have been injured or killed.

Race officials did not notice the infraction, but Julie knew she had to stand her ground and let the other jockey know he could not bully her. She refused to be intimidated. As she once explained, "The weak ones get weeded out." When the jockey weighed out after the race, Julie confronted him. He barely looked at her and muttered that it had been an accident. Julie didn't believe him and shoved him off the scales and onto the ground. The jockey never struck her horse again. On another occasion, she fought a male jockey after she believed he had made a dangerous move on the track. In the worst incident of all, another jockey slashed his whip across Julie's face during a race, cutting her ear. After the race, Julie stormed after the jockey, and before he could react, she punched him right in the nose! He responded by pushing her into the jockeys' swimming pool. Dripping wet, Julie climbed out and hit him with a lounge chair. Both Julie and the other jockey were fined and suspended, but Julie had made her point. If challenged, she would fight back. By standing up for herself—and by winning races—she slowly earned the respect of not only the jockeys but also the trainers and owners of the horses.

After only a few years, Julie had become one of the best and best known jockeys in the country. In 1987 she became the first female jockey to be the leading winner at a major track with 130 wins at Monmouth, New Jersey. Over the next few years, she added more track titles. In 1992, Julie led all riders at Belmont Park in Belmont, New York, site of the Belmont Stakes. Julie's horses won the ninth most money in horse racing that year, more than nine million dollars. Julie received a percentage of each winning purse and became very wealthy. She was easily the most successful woman jockey in the history of racing.

Despite all her success, one thing had eluded her. She had raced in the Belmont Stakes in both 1991 and 1992 and in the Kentucky Derby in 1992, but her horses had not been good enough to win. Although she told one interviewer that "I'd like to win the classic races," meaning one of the Triple Crown events, she added, "Riding in them is no big deal to me." But Julie really did not believe that. Despite all her victories, she knew that until she won one of horseracing's most prestigious events, some people would continue to think that women did not belong in racing, that they simply were not as good as men. After her losses in her first few Triple Crown events, some track insiders whispered that women jockeys like Julie simply were not strong enough to ride a horse to victory in a Triple Crown race, where jockeys had to push and muscle their horses to perform their absolute very best.

In 1992 she had had the opportunity to ride a horse named Colonial Affair. A little stubborn, and full of life, Colonial Affair reminded Julie of Filly. The horse seemed to respond to Julie and ran better for her than for other jockeys. Colonial Affair's trainer, Scotty Schulhofer, recognized that and observed that Julie "has got a great feel for horses. . . . they just respond to her."

Although Colonial Affair's owner did not race his horse in either the 1993 Kentucky Derby or the Preakness, he decided to enter Colonial Affair in the last race of the Triple

Crown, the Belmont Stakes. The longest of the three Triple Crown races, at one and a half miles, the Belmont is known as the Test of Champions. Many terrific horses, unaccustomed to running a mile and a half, fail in the Belmont.

As the day of the race approached, Julie had a good feeling, both about her horse and about herself. Scotty Schulhofer believed in her, telling her, "They say you can't win the big ones, but this is just another race....Be patient. You can do it."

Julie thought she could as well. For the first time ever, she felt as if she had a horse with the ability and the heart to win a Triple Crown race. Since she had met Colonial Affair, the horse had filled out, growing from a young colt into a powerful and athletic horse. Yet Colonial Affair still retained the same determined personality that reminded Julie of Filly. He liked to goof around in the paddock, but once it was time to race, all he wanted to do was run.

A few days before the race, Julie received a letter from her mother. Judi reminded her daughter how they used to watch the Triple Crown races together, writing, "You used to say, 'Someday that's gonna be me out there!' Well, honey, today's the day....Not many people grow up and actually live the dreams they had as kids." That was exactly what Julie was determined to do.

The day of the race, Julie got up early and went to the barn to see Colonial Affair. The horse was already awake and alert, as if he knew that this was a big day. He oozed confidence.

So did Julie. That morning she bumped into a former jockey who had once won the Belmont himself, and she asked him boldly, "What's it going to feel like when I have that blanket of carnations in my lap at the winner's circle?" She told her assistant, "I'm really going to do it," and asked him to make sure he got some extra programs so she could keep them as souvenirs.

A short time before the race, Julie made her way to the saddling paddock. She mounted Colonial Affair and then leaned over and patted the huge horse on his neck. "Let's go out and make some history," she said.

As Colonial Affair and the other horses made their way to the starting gate in the post parade, Julie liked the lively way her horse pranced around, as if he were a king and all the other horses were his subjects. But apart from Julie, not many other people had much faith in Colonial Affair. The favorites were Sea Hero, winner of the Kentucky Derby, and Prairie Bayou, winner of the Preakness. The odds on Colonial Affair winning the race were only fourteen to one.

As Colonial Affair entered the starting gate in the fourth

position from the rail, Julie went over the race in her mind. Prairie Bayou was right next to her, while Sea Horse was farther outside. It was drizzling, and the track was wet. With fourteen horses in the race, Julie knew it would be crowded at the start. She also knew that Colonial Affair didn't really like to run with mud flying off other horses' hooves into his face. She planned to follow Scotty's advice: be patient at the start and stay out of trouble. In another two and half minutes, she would learn whether her strategy had paid off.

At the bell, Colonial Affair got off to a quick, clean start. Julie did not push him. She allowed other horses and riders to vie for the lead and let Colonial Affair run comfortably. She settled in on the inside, ten or twelve lengths back.

Because of the track conditions, the pace was relatively slow, and Julie was content to stay back through the first turn and into the backstretch. But as Colonial Affair approached the midpoint of the race, Julie's years of experience told her that her horse was getting frustrated. Riding near the rail on the inside of the track, Colonial Affair was getting crowded, and mud was flying in their faces.

Julie paid close attention to the horses around her. She wanted to move to the outside away from the mud and traffic. It would be slightly farther around the track, but she sensed that Colonial Affair would run faster with a bit more room, and she let a few horses pass until her horse was in the clear.

As one horse passed her on the outside, Julie saw that she had an opportunity to make her move. She barely tugged on the reins, giving Colonial Affair the signal to move.

The horse immediately responded, gliding to the out-side without slowing down, drifting out of traffic and away from the mud. Although Colonial Affair was still ten or twelve lengths from the lead and in ninth or tenth place, Julie was not worried. There was a lot of race left to run. All of a sudden she could feel Colonial Affair relax and begin to race strongly again.

Through her mud-splattered goggles, Julie kept her eye on race favorite Sea Hero. At the end of the backstretch, she pushed her horse a bit harder and Colonial Affair in-creased his speed, easily passing several horses. With each stride, he drew closer to Sea Hero.

They pulled alongside the horse, and just as they en-tered the final turn, Colonial Affair drew ahead.

Now there were only four horses ahead of Julie and Colonial Affair. Staying wide through the turn, she resisted the urge to push Colonial Affair to the front. Her years of experience told her that some of the horses ahead of her would soon start to fade. Meanwhile, Colonial Affair was still running strong.

Sure enough, as they moved through the turn, the pack of horses in the lead all began to falter. As they came out of the turn, Colonial Affair was running as if he were going downhill, while all the others were running as if racing up a steep slope. Gaining ground with each stride, he surged past the other horses on the outside. With two furlongs, or a quarter mile, remaining, he pulled into the lead.

Now Julie began pushing her horse, urging Colonial Affair to stretch out and run hard through the finish. With one-eighth of a mile to go, he was in front and in the clear. Julie hardly had to use the whip at all as Colonial Affair thundered toward the finish line. Now mud was flying off his hooves and spraying the other horses.

Victory! Julie and Colonial Affair crossed the finish line two and one-quarter lengths ahead of any other horse. As she eased up on the reins and Colonial Affair began to slow down, Julie was almost speechless. By the time she reached the winner's circle and the carpet of carnations was placed across her lap, her accomplishment had begun to sink in.

Of course someone asked her how it felt to be the first woman to win a Triple Crown race. She responded thoughtfully. She did not just want to be considered a great female jockey. She wanted to be considered a great jockey, period. "I don't think the question needs to be genderized," she said. "It would feel great to anyone. But whether you're a girl or a boy or a Martian, you still have to go out and prove yourself every day."

And that is just what Julie Krone had done every single day since she had first decided to pursue her dream. It hardly seemed possible, but she had gone from spending her days dreaming about horses to fulfilling her dream.

A short time later she called her mother. Even though Julie preferred not to talk about it, being the first woman to win a Triple Crown race felt pretty good. Because of her, other female jockeys know that there are no limits to what they can accomplish.

"I'm on the ceiling," her mother told her. "Come scrape me off!" The sport of kings was now also the sport of queens. Julie Krone was wearing the crown.

Danica Patrick shows off her trophy after winning the Japan 300 at the Twin Ring Motegi track in Japan. Her victory was the first by a woman in an Indy car race.

YOUNG WOMAN
IN A HURRY

As THE POWDER BLUE NUMBER SEVEN CAR hurtled into the final turn at nearly two hundred miles per hour, the driver stayed focused. Hands wrapped securely around the steering wheel, the driver deftly made a slight turn to the left, and the car, a low-slung Indy-style racer with an open cockpit, rocketed down low along the track's edge; then, as the turn ended and the driver pressed the accelerator, the car shot out of the turn into the homestretch only a few inches from the barricade that separated the track from thousands of cheering fans.

The driver heard none of this. In the hot, cramped cockpit, peering out from behind the visor of a helmet and dripping with sweat inside a fireproof jumpsuit, the driver of the car was looking far down the track toward the finish line, trying to anticipate trouble before it was too late to react to it.

The driver began to make out the waving of a checkered flag far ahead, but getting closer every millisecond. In another second or two, this race would end.

Victory had been a long time coming. For more than a decade, ever since the driver first climbed into a go-kart, winning a big race in an Indy-style racer was all she had ever wanted to do.

That's right — *she*. Because as the checkered flag flashed before her eyes and Danica Patrick won her first race in an Indy car, she knew that, at long last, she had proven wrong everyone who believed that a woman could never, ever, *ever* win an Indy car race against a field of men.

As she eased back on the throttle and began her victory lap, Danica Patrick began to smile.

Thwack!

T. J. Patrick cringed when he saw the go-kart smack into the concrete wall. He was already sprinting toward the car as his ten-year-old daughter, Danica, tumbled from the cockpit and sprawled upon the ground. Her first time in her brand-new kart, Danica had crashed.

Getting his daughters go-karts had seemed like a great idea to T.J. Eight-year-old Brooke had been begging for one for years, and Danica had recently decided she wanted one, too. The girls looked up to their father, who ran a plate-glass business and a coffee shop but still managed to find time to race. Over the years, T.J. had raced nearly every kind of vehicle that existed, from go-karts and motorcycles to snowmobiles. In fact, he met the girls' mother, his wife, Bev, on a blind date at a snowmobile race. She had been a mechanic for another driver.

Earlier that cold March day in Rockford, Illinois, T.J. had taken the girls and their karts to an empty parking lot next to his glass store. He had carefully laid out an oval racecourse, using empty paint cans to mark the edge of the "track."

Although some racing go-karts are complicated machines that can go well over one hundred miles an hour, the girls' were very simple. Sitting low to the ground, each was powered by a small engine. The karts' top speed was about twenty-five miles an hour, plenty fast for two young girls, and were very easy to operate. Compared to a full-size racing car, they were also relatively safe. One pedal operated the brake and another the accelerator. All the girls had to do was steer and keep from crashing into one another — or something else.

T.J. spent a few minutes explaining to the impatient young girls how to operate the karts, then made them put on safety helmets. T.J. adjusted the helmets and the girls climbed into the cars and took off.

Neither Danica nor Brooke thought there was anything strange about what they were doing. They had grown up around racing but had never noticed that virtually every driver at every race was male. They had no idea that they were probably the only two girls at their school who wanted to race go-karts.

The girls steered carefully onto the track and accelerated, the karts jumping forward and then slowing down as each girl became accustomed to the feel of the accelerator pedal. Then Danica pushed the pedal toward the ground and her car took off.

She loved it. Even though the March air felt chilly in the open cockpit, Danica barely noticed. Sitting just a few inches off the ground made twenty-five miles per hour feel like two hundred.

As she approached the paint cans marking out the first turn, she remembered what her father had taught her. She took her foot off the accelerator and tapped gently on the brake. He had told her that it was safer to brake before the turn and then accelerate as she came out of it — and that she'd go faster that way.

Danica performed the maneuver perfectly. With each lap she became a little more confident.

But on her fifth lap, Danica tapped the brake and the car failed to slow. Something was wrong! Danica pushed the brake pedal all the way down, but the go-kart didn't respond. She held tight to the steering wheel; she didn't know what to do.

The little kart sped by the paint cans and kept going straight, directly toward the back end of a parked tractor-trailer! T.J. saw what was about to happen and starting running toward his daughter. It seemed certain that Danica's head would strike the bottom edge of the trailer.

At the last second, Danica instinctively swerved. Instead of striking the trailer, the kart hit the wall of her father's building with a sickening thud. Danica's body smacked against the steering wheel, and she was thrown from her seat to the ground. Although the engine stopped, her coat came into contact with the motor and caught fire. Danica didn't move.

In a flash, T.J. beat out the flames and pulled Danica from the crumpled kart. Brooke watched as T.J. held Danica's limp body in his hands. For moment or two Danica didn't move. Then she blinked a few times and looked up.

She was shaken, but she was okay. T.J. let out a huge sigh of relief. He examined the kart and discovered that the accident had been his fault. The last time he had been working on the kart, he had left a pin out, and that had caused the brakes to fail.

He felt terrible. He figured the last thing Danica would ever want to do was get into a go-kart again.

But Danica understood that the accident had not been her fault—the kart had simply malfunctioned. She didn't like crashing, but she loved the feeling of going fast.

She wanted to keep racing... as soon as the brakes were fixed!

By the start of summer, Danica and Brooke were pestering their parents to let them do some real racing. An organization called the World Karting Association (WKA) sponsors go-kart races all around the world that match drivers of various ages and abilities. The WKA enforces safety rules, such as requiring drivers to wear helmets and seat harnesses, and makes sure the sport is as safe as possible, so T.J. and Bev agreed to allow their daughters to race. But T.J. didn't just push his daughters out onto the track. As he later told a reporter, "I made a rule that if [Danica] was going to do this, she had to learn something every time she went onto the track. She had to learn how to tune her own carburetor and understand things like when her tires were going bad."

Both Danica and Brooke learned fast. They quickly realized that at most races, they were not only among the youngest competitors, but also the only girls on the track. Most of their opponents were teenage boys and young men, none of whom wanted to lose to a girl, particularly to girls like Brooke and Danica, both of whom were only about four feet tall and weighed around fifty pounds. But the other drivers soon learned that it didn't matter how old or how big Danica and her sister were. On a racetrack the only thing that matters is how well a person drives and how much he or she wants to win. And Danica wanted to win. She was in a hurry.

Not that the boys made it easy for her or her sister. They did not. They tried to intimidate the girls both on and off the track. Before the races few of the other drivers ever spoke to the girls or even looked their way except to mutter something nasty. On the track the girls were treated even worse. The other drivers would gang up on Danica and Brooke and do their best to keep either girl from winning. If one of the girls tried to pass another kart, another driver often would get in the way and force them to slow down. Sometime the drivers would even try to bump into one of the Patrick girls' cars and force them off the track.

Even though Brooke had initially been more eager to race than Danica, she soon grew tired of all the rough driving and told her father she didn't want to race anymore. But Danica had a different reaction.

Although she lost badly at first, she followed her father's advice and tried to learn something in every race. Even though she was small and young, she improved each time she got on the track. She quickly understood that to win a race, a driver not only had to race well, but also had to drive smart. Danica spent as much time as her father working on her kart and making small mechanical adjustments to get it to go just a little faster.

Danica soon discovered that she had quicker reactions than many other drivers. She was able to steer her car through tight spots, then accelerate past the competition before they even realized she was there. She learned to drive what is known as a "clean line," taking the shortest and fastest route around the track, the one that requires the least amount of steering and braking. She also learned to "draft" behind other karts, allowing them to cut through the wind ahead of her before she pulled out and then slingshot past them.

It wasn't long before Danica began making her mark. She won races and set records for her age at track after track. Only three months into her career, she set a track record for all age groups at a racecourse in Wisconsin, and at her local track she finished her first season second in the overall standings.

With the support of her family, Danica was soon spending almost every weekend racing go-karts. Although she was still usually the only woman racing, she wasn't intimidated. If anyone was intimidated, it was the boys she raced against. She developed a reputation for smart, aggressive driving and for going all out to win.

One of her rivals was a young racer named Sam Hornish, Jr. Three years older than Danica, Hornish would later go on to race Indy cars; in 2006 he would win the Indianapolis 500. For now, he was one of the best kart racers around. Danica *hated* losing to Hornish.

In one race when she was thirteen years old, she lost

an early heat to Hornish. When they raced again later that day, Danica entered the final turn in second place, just a few yards behind Hornish. Hornish, protecting his lead, eased off the accelerator, trying to force Danica to slow down as well and making it impossible to pass him.

But the instant she saw his car slow, she gritted her teeth and hit the accelerator hard with her foot. All of a sudden his car was right in front of her. Danica didn't have time to stop.

Danica's car hit Hornish's car and then ran right over the top of it and went flying through the air. Fortunately, no one was hurt, but as Danica commented later, "I was totally going for the win.... I think I scared the boys, including Sam."

As she racked up win after win on the go-kart circuit, she began to attract attention and sponsorship from companies that made engines, tires, and other equipment. With sponsorship she was able to spend the money to make mechanical improvements to her kart that allowed her to go faster and win even more often.

Off the track she looked like any other teenager, but on the track she was a tiger. In only three years she advanced from participating in regional races to racing in events that attracted the best drivers from all over the nation. In 1996 she won an incredible thirty-nine of forty-nine races in her class, and between 1994 and 1997, Danica won three WKA Grand National Championships.

A generation earlier, a driver named Lyn St. James became one of the first women to race Indy-style cars. Danica dreamed of following St. James onto the track and racing cars for a living herself one day. When Danica was fourteen, she attended a two-day driver development program for girls sponsored by St. James. As St. James later recalled, "It became obvious that she was special." St. James had never met a fourteen year old—male or female—who had Danica's combination of talent and desire, as well as a supportive family. St. James knew better than anyone just how hard it was for a woman to make it in racing, but she believed in Danica and stayed in touch with her. She invited Danica to attend the Indianapolis 500, the biggest and most famous Indy car race in the world, a grueling five-hundred-mile race held each Memorial Day at the historic Indianapolis Motor Speedway.

But racing in the Indy 500 was a dream that Danica didn't even dare to dream. Racing go-karts was expensive enough; it cost millions of dollars to put together an Indy racing car. Only the best drivers in the world are able to attract sponsors with the money it takes to be competitive.

When Danica was sixteen, St. James introduced her and her family to John Mecom III, a wealthy Texan who enjoyed sponsoring drivers. He had already heard of Patrick and was intrigued by the idea of a woman racing Indy cars. He told her family that if Danica wanted to continue her career, she should do so in England in the Formula Vauxhall series, which features cars similar to those used in Indy car racing. Many drivers use the Vauxhall series to prepare themselves to drive Indy cars.

Mecom thought Danica had a future as a driver and offered to sponsor her to race in England. "You'll learn more over there in one year," said Mecom, "than you will in five in the States."

Danica's family was hesitant, but Danica was not. Even though she would have to drop out of high school and give up cheerleading and other school activities, she desperately wanted to continue her racing career and thought the opportunity to go to England was too good to pass up.

Her parents reluctantly agreed. "If you want to be the best lawyer, you go to Harvard," her mother explained later, "and if you want to be the best driver, you go to England."

Danica spent most of the next four years in England,

racing every weekend, earning a high school diploma, and living in a small room in the home of a family she hardly knew. It was a tough life. Not only did she have to adapt to a different culture and make new friends, but she had to learn to race an entirely different kind of car. The competition was much stiffer than on the go-kart circuit, and few of the other drivers — all men — were nice to her. Moreover, after only a year, Mecom withdrew his support. For a time, until the Ford Motor Company decided to help out, Danica's family had to pay her way. It was a struggle, but Danica got a little better every year. In 2001 she was named the top prospect in the Formula Vauxhall racing circuit in England.

It was time to come home.

Danica wanted to race Indy cars more than ever, but that still seemed a distant dream. Fortunately, Bobby Rahal, an American who had won the 1986 Indianapolis 500 before retiring, was putting together a racing team. He knew of Danica from her time racing go-karts and had seen her race in England. He not only thought she was a good driver, he also thought her good looks and personality would attract attention to the sport. He invited Danica to join Team Rahal and in 2003 sponsored her in the Toyota Atlantic Series, a racing series just one step below the Indy

Racing League (IRL), the top Indy car racing circuit in the United States.

She did not disappoint him. In 2004, her second year in the series, she finished in the top five in ten of twelve races and finished third in the overall standings. Rahal was impressed and announced that in 2005 he planned to have Patrick race in the IRL and would enter her in the Indianapolis 500.

Danica was thrilled. And so was everyone else — well, almost everyone.

At age twenty-three, Danica became a celebrity almost overnight. Although there had been a few female race-car drivers before, none were as young and attractive as Danica. She stood barely five feet tall and weighed just over a hundred pounds. With her long, straight dark hair and pixie-ish features, Danica looked more like an actress or a model than a racecar driver. It hardly seemed possible that someone so small could drive a car weighing thousands of pounds powered by an enormous engine. Before she had even participated in an Indy race, she was the subject of dozens of magazine and newspaper articles, and companies selling everything from clothes to shampoo were signing her up for lucrative endorsement contracts.

Some male drivers saw all the attention she was getting and became jealous. They believed she wasn't that talented and that if she were not so attractive, she never would have been put behind the wheel of a racecar. Richard Petty, one of the greatest drivers in NASCAR history, summed up the feelings of many male fans and drivers when he said bluntly, "I just don't think [racing is] a sport for women." But other men were more accepting. Her old rival Sam Hornish Jr. said, "She's not just talented, but she's the best-looking racer we've had as well — not to make the women who went before her mad. She's a very marketable package." Hornish knew that Danica would attract more fans to racing, which would be good for the sport. Still, Danica knew that until she actually won a race, there would be people who believed that women had no place on the racetrack.

"I want people to say, 'You're a good driver,' not 'You're a good female,'" she told a reporter. "I know I'm the best chick."

Danica's performance in her first Indy 500 answered the question of whether or not she was a good driver. In qualifying practice leading up to the race, Danica turned in the fastest lap of any driver, timed at the incredible speed of 229.88 miles per hour, and qualified fourth among all drivers and began the race in the second row.

From the moment the starter of the race called out "Lady and gentlemen, start your engines," Danica raced strategically, driving to win. At first she drove conservatively, not wanting to risk an accident early in the race when the track was crowded with thirty-three cars. She knew that the 500, a race of five hundred miles on a track two and a half miles long, required patience. It didn't matter what place she was in early in the race. All that mattered was where she finished.

But her car was so fast that for a short time, as drivers ahead of her left the track to refuel, she found herself in first place. Then she stopped to refuel herself and spent the middle part of the race stalking the lead drivers and trying to stay out of trouble.

At lap 143 Danica roared into the pits, where her team of mechanics waited, and topped off her gas tank. If everything went according to plan, she would not need to stop again before the end of the race. Team leader Bobby Rahal knew Danica was taking a risk. If she ran out of gas, she wouldn't win. But if the gamble paid off and Danica was able to stay on the track when others ahead of her had to stop for more fuel, well, she just might sneak into first place.

Danica was near the end of a long line of cars on lap 172 when one car after another pulled off the track ahead of her and into pit row for more fuel. Danica simply kept her foot on the accelerator and kept going. When she passed pit row, all she saw was open track ahead of her. She was in first place! If she could hold on for another twenty-eight laps — another seventy miles — she would win the Indy 500.

After only a few seconds, the other cars pulled back onto the track and chased Danica. Her car was fast, but it was not the fastest on the track, and she had to drive carefully to make her fuel last. If she sped up and slowed down needlessly, she would waste fuel.

Lap after lap, as the crowd at the speedway roared over the sound of the engines, Danica clung to her lead. But with each lap, her competition pulled a little closer.

Danica did everything she could, but it was impossible to hold off everyone. Only a few laps from the finish, she was passed by Dan Wheldon. His car was simply running faster than hers. Rather than fight a hopeless battle and risk running out of fuel, Danica settled in behind another car to conserve gas and make sure she finished the race When she saw the checkered flag and crossed the finish line, she was in fourth place.

It wasn't as good as first place, but it was good enough to get everyone's attention. No woman had ever finished so near the lead in any Indy car race, not to mention in the

Indy 500. Danica proved that she was talented enough to-compete on the Indy car circuit. It looked like just a matter of time before Danica got to take her victory lap.

Although Danica raced well for the remainder of the 2005 season and was named the IndyCar Series Rookie of the Year, victory proved to be elusive. Sometimes she raced well only to be thwarted by mechanical problems with her car, and sometimes she made foolish mistakes that took her out of the running. Although she finished twelfth in the points standing in 2005 and ninth in 2006, with an eighth-place finish in the Indy 500, some other drivers and racing fans were still whispering that Danica didn't have what it took to be a winner, and that she really wasn't a very good driver. Danica knew that those whispers would continue until she won a race.

In 2007 she changed teams, joining the Andretti Green team. Her performance improved, and she finished in the top five in four different races and ended the season seventh in the points standings. But she still hadn't won a race.

In May of 2008 she traveled to Japan for the Indy Japan 300 at the 1.5-mile Twin Ring Motegi racecourse. Before the race a reporter asked her, "What is it going to take for you to put this car in victory lane today?"

Danica hesitated. Her car had not been running very

well. She had had a hard time even qualifying for the race.

"I'm guessing," she said, "I'm just going to have to find that calculated balance between pushing hard enough to stay in front, but smart enough to finish." Then, anticipating his next question, she addressed the way she felt about not yet having won a race.

"It's frustrating," she said. "I just wish it would be over with."

Early in the race, Danica struggled to find that balance. On lap 143 of the 200-lap race, she pulled into the pits with a few other cars to top off her gas tank. The announcer for the broadcast back to the United States called the move "a calculated risk." It was. Danica and a few other drivers had decided to try to run the rest of the race without stopping for any more fuel. If it worked, it could mean victory. If not, Danica would have to answer the same old questions once again.

Back on the track, Danica hung with the lead group of drivers, drafting behind other cars to save fuel and keep them within reach without pushing her car too hard. She knew that it didn't matter how far ahead she was as long as she finished first. With only a few laps to go, her strategy started to pay off. Car after car after car had to pull into pit row for more gas. All of a sudden, Danica found herself in second place behind the white and orange car of veteran driver Helio Castroneves.

Castroneves was not just another driver hoping to win. He was widely recognized as one of the best Indy car drivers in the world and had already won the Indy 500 twice. Danica knew he would not make a mistake. She wasn't going to win by accident. She would have to beat him.

And Castroneves knew he was in for a battle. Before the race he had been asked about Danica's chances, and unlike some drivers in the race, he had admitted that he respected her ability.

"Danica has as good a shot as anyone," he told a reporter. "She no longer overdrives her car. If her car is bad, she won't push it and wreck. But if her car is good, she'll get everything she can out of it. She's really grown."

Over the next few minutes, Danica proved Castroneves correct. She stayed close behind him for a few laps and then decided to make her move. As the two cars stormed down the backstretch two and a half laps from the finish, Danica sensed that if she drove smart, she had enough fuel to win. But she knew that she probably had only enough fuel to make one attempt to pass Castroneves. If her attempt failed, not only would she run out of gas and lose the race, but she would probably be ridiculed for making a poor decision.

Everyone who still believed that women should not be race-car drivers would point to her failure as evidence.

As the two cars rocketed down the backstretch only a few feet apart, Danica slowly accelerated and drew her powder blue number seven car toward Castroneves's back bumper. Then she began to pull out on his right side, paying close attention to see whether he would try to block her.

Castroneves was low on fuel, too. He hesitated, and as he did, Danica put more pressure on her gas pedal. The car responded with a roar. Danica shot past her opponent. Then, as the two cars entered the next turn, she cut her wheel and dropped down in front of the veteran driver.

Castroneves knew that when he had hesitated earlier, he had lost the race. Now he didn't have enough gas to stay with Danica and attempt to pass her. He eased up on the accelerator and let her go. He had been outsmarted — and outdriven.

With less than two laps remaining in the race, Danica stayed focused and made sure she drove a clean line. This was no time to get overconfident. She still had to conserve fuel, and she was still going more than two hundred miles an hour. Any mistake could be disastrous.

Finally, she saw a race official waving the white flag that marked the beginning of the final lap. Danica was all by herself. Castroneves's car was far behind, and she had nothing but a wide-open track ahead of her.

Danica wasn't in a hurry, but she could hardly wait. The stands flashed by in a blur, and she tried not to think about what it all meant. In pit row, her mother, Bev, raised her arms over her head and screamed in celebration.

But Danica could not celebrate — not yet. She tried to keep her emotions in check on the final lap. It seemed to take forever. Finally, as she rounded the final turn and saw the checkered flag, she allowed herself to begin to relax. A race official waved the flag in the air, and Danica rocketed past it and eased off the gas pedal. A faint smile formed on her face as she thought back to the first time she had ever driven a go-kart, when she'd lost her brakes. She remembered her battles with Sam Hornish Jr. and the long, lonely days in England. By the time she completed her victory lap, climbed out of her car, and pulled off her helmet, she was crying tears of joy.

She paused and looked around as her crew and family offered their congratulations. From now on, no one would ever, ever question whether Danica or any woman could drive an Indy car as well as a man.

She let out a big sigh and smiled.

"It's been," she said of her victory, "a long time coming."

SOURCES AND FURTHER READING

I use many sources when writing a book, including newspapers, magazines, books, interviews, video documentaries, and the Internet.

If you would like to read more about any of the athletes in this book, ask your teacher or your school or town librarian to show you how to find newspaper and magazine articles online. You might also want to check out the books and articles listed below, many of which were helpful to me. The books may be purchased online or at any bookstore. They might also be in your local library. If not, your library can probably borrow them for you from another library.

Don't be afraid to ask your librarian or your teacher for help, and happy reading!

TRUDY EDERLE

America's Champion Swimmer, by David A. Adler. Harcourt, 2000. This is a terrific illustrated book for younger children.

Young Woman and the Sea: How Trudy Ederle Conquered the English Channel and Inspired the World, by Glenn Stout. Houghton Mifflin Harcourt, 2009.

You can find newsreel footage of Trudy swimming in the English Channel on YouTube.

LOUISE STOKES AND TIDYE PICKETT

No one has ever written a book about Louise or Tidye. In fact, the story in this book about the two young women is the most extensive ever published. In September of 1988 I wrote an article about Louise titled "Off Track" for *Boston Magazine*. To write the article, I did a great deal of research in newspapers. I also spoke to Louise's sister, Emily, and to sportswriter Mabray "Doc" Kountze, who knew Louise well. A great article on Louise titled "Nowhere, Fast," by Bob Duffy, appeared in the *Boston Globe* newspaper on September 10, 2000. The best article I found about Tidye appeared in the *Chicago Tribune* on August 10, 1984: "Pioneer from 1932 Remains Undaunted," by Jody Homer.

Their Day in the Sun: Women of the 1932 Olympics, by Doris H. Pieroth. The University of Washington Press, 1996.

If you enjoyed reading about Tidye and Louise, you might also enjoy reading about these African American sports pioneers:

Jesse Owens (track)

Wilma Rudolph (track)

Althea Gibson (tennis)

Jackie Robinson (baseball)

JULIE KRONE

Riding for My Life, by Julie Krone with Nancy Ann Richardson. Little, Brown and Company, 1995. There may soon be a movie based on this book!

Great Women in the Sport of Kings: America's Top Women Jockeys Tell Their Stories, edited by Scooter Toby Davidson and Valerie Anthony. Syracuse University Press, 1999.

You can look up Julie's victory at the Belmont, or her performances in other races, on YouTube.

DANICA PATRICK

Danica is the subject of nearly a dozen books. You may want to start with her autobiography:

Danica: Crossing the Line, by Danica Patrick with Laura Morton. Simon and Schuster, 2006.

You can look up Danica's first win on YouTube.

ABOUT THE AUTHOR

When Glenn Stout was growing up outside a small town in central Ohio, he never dreamed that he would become a writer. Then reading changed his life. As a kid, Glenn played baseball, basketball, and football, but baseball was always his favorite sport. Glenn studied poetry and creative writing in college and has had many different jobs, including selling minor league baseball tickets, cleaning offices, grading papers for a college, and painting houses. He also worked as a construction worker and a librarian. Glenn started writing professionally while he was working at the Boston Public Library and has been a full-time writer since 1993. Under the auspices of Matt Christopher, Glenn wrote forty titles in the Matt Christopher sports biography series, and every year he edits *The Best American Sports Writing* collection. Some of Glenn's other books include *Red Sox Century, Yankees Century, Nine Months at Ground Zero,* and *Young Woman and the Sea: How Trudy Ederle Conquered the English Channel and Inspired the World.* He has written or edited more than seventy books.

Glenn is a citizen of both the United States and Canada and lives on Lake Champlain in Vermont with his wife, daughter, three cats, two dogs, and a rabbit. He writes in a messy office in his basement, and when he isn't working, he likes to ski, skate, hike in the woods, kayak on the lake, take photographs, and read.

APPENDIX

GERTRUDE "TRUDY" EDERLE

BORN: October 23, 1905, in New York, New York.

DIED: November 30, 2003, in Wyckoff, New Jersey.

Member of United States Women's Olympic team, 1924.

Winner of a gold medal as one of four members of the
400-meter freestyle relay team.

Winner of a bronze medal in both the 100-meter and
400-meter individual freestyle races.

First woman to swim the English Channel.

MAE LOUISE STOKES (FRASER)

BORN: October 27, 1913, in Malden, Massachusetts.

DIED: March 25, 1978, in Boston, Massachusetts.

Member of United States Women's Olympic teams, 1932
and 1936.

THEODORA ANN "TIDYE" PICKETT (PHILLIPS)

BORN: November 3, 1914, in Chicago, Illinois.

DIED: November 17, 1986, in Chicago Heights, Illinois.

Member of United States Women's Olympic teams, 1932
and 1936.

JULIEANN LOUISE KRONE

BORN: July 24, 1963, Benton Harbor, Michigan.

First female jockey to win riding championships at
Belmont Park, Gulfstream Park, Monmouth Park, the
Meadowlands, and Atlantic City Race Course.
First female jockey to win a Triple Crown race (1993
Belmont Stakes, aboard Colonial Affair).
First woman inducted into the National Museum of
Racing and Hall of Fame, 2000.

DANICA PATRICK

BORN: March 25, 1982, Beloit, Wisconsin.

Indianapolis 500 Rookie of the Year, 2005.
IndyCar Series Rookie of the Year, 2005.
Fourth woman to race in the Indianapolis 500.
First woman to win an Indy Racing League series event.
Racing Record, 2004–2009:

RACES	WINNER OF POLE	WINS	TOP 10S
81	3	1	41

DON'T MISS THE FIRST BOOK

GOOD ★ SPORTS

BY GLENN STOUT

BASEBALL HEROES

Featuring:

GREENBERG   VALENZUELA   BORDERS   and   ROBINSON

IN THE GOOD SPORTS SERIES!

Every athlete has a story. Even professionals were kids once, playing sports for fun. On the way to achieving their dream, some faced obstacles so big, people said they couldn't surmount them. But they persevered, overcoming everything placed in their paths.

JACKIE ROBINSON was the first African American player in the major leagues.

HANK GREENBERG opened the door for Jewish American ballplayers.

FERNANDO VALENZUELA became the first Mexican superstar and opened baseball up to Latin American fans.

ILA BORDERS showed that a girl can be good enough to play with the boys.

YES, THEY DID!

MORE TRUE STORIES

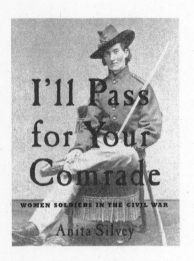

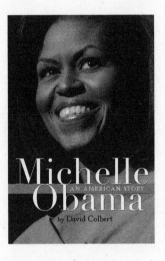

I'LL PASS FOR YOUR
COMRADE
Explore the fascinating secret
world of women soldiers in the
Civil War: who they were, why
they went to war, how they
managed their masquerade.

MICHELLE OBAMA:
AN AMERICAN STORY
The First Lady's life story, and
how it was affected by African American history: slavery,
freedom, the Reconstruction
era, Jim Crow, life in northern industrial cities, the civil
rights movement, and finally
her own era.

ABOUT TRULY AMAZING WOMEN

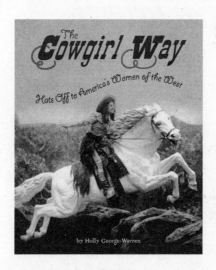

THE COWGIRL WAY

Welcome to the world of the cowgirl! They were nimble equestriennes, hawkeyed sharp-shooters, sly outlaws, eloquent legislators, expert wranglers, and talented performers who made eyes pop and jaws drop with their skills, savvy, and bravery.

FIND MORE FUN AND FUNNY
BIOGRAPHIES IN THE LIVES
OF . . . SERIES BY KATHLEEN
KRULL, ILLUSTRATED BY
KATHRYN HEWITT:

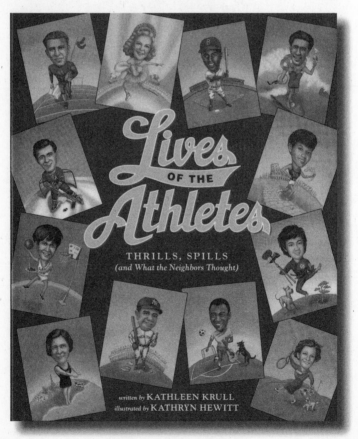

LIVES OF THE ATHLETES

LIVES OF THE ARTISTS

LIVES OF THE MUSICIANS

LIVES OF THE PRESIDENTS

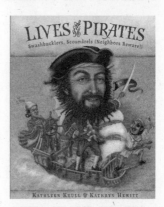

LIVES OF THE PIRATES

LIVES OF THE WRITERS

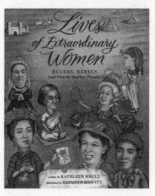

LIVES OF EXTRAORDINARY WOMEN

FACT OR FICTION? READ THESE AWESOME NOVELS ABOUT SPORTS AND ATHLETES.

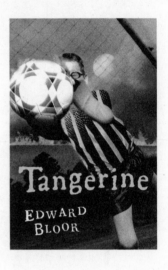

PEAK

The emotional, tension-filled story of a fourteen-year-old boy's attempt to be the youngest person to reach the top of Mount Everest.

TANGERINE

In Tangerine County, Florida, weird is normal. Lightning strikes at the same time every day, a sinkhole swallows a local school, and Paul the geek finds himself adopted into the toughest group around: the middle school soccer team.

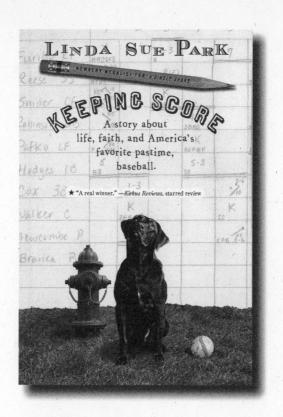

KEEPING SCORE

Nine-year-old Maggie learns a lot about baseball and life in this historical novel set during the Korean War and the Dodgers' 1951 season.